The Rise and Decline
of
President Gloria Macapagal-Arroyo

The Rise and Decline
of
President Gloria Macapagal-Arroyo

By
Patricio R. Mamot, Ph.D.

E-BookTime, LLC
Montgomery, Alabama

The Rise and Decline of
President Gloria Macapagal-Arroyo

ISBN: 978-1-59824-777-0

First Edition
Published March 2008
E-BookTime, LLC
6598 Pumpkin Road
Montgomery, AL 36108
www.e-booktime.com

Dedication

To more than 11 million overseas Filipino workers (OFWs) – the modern-day heroes of the Philippines – whose annual remittance of US$15 billion sustains our economy plagued with corruption under Pres. Arroyo's watch.

Contents

Contents

Contents

Introduction
By Jose Mari Mercader

"Pres. Arroyo is even more corrupt than the disgraced Pres. Ferdinand E. Marcos." *Pulse Asia, January 2008*

Power intoxicates. The greater the power the greater the intoxication (Ang kapangyarihan ay nakakaka lasing). This truism is seen in the panorama of contemptuous abuses committed by those in high places in the government. If there is someone to blame for the excesses in our current government, it should be Pres. Arroyo herself because leadership is by example.

The stigma of our country being known as one of the most corrupt nations in the world - first in Asia - compels Dr. Patricio R. Mamot to carry a crusade in his hard-hitting columns and editorials at the Filipino Times in New York in the hope of sending the message that Pres. Arroyo cannot continue abusing human rights and indulging in wanton corruption with impunity because there are concerned citizens even from afar (USA) who are reporting to the world that in the Philippines Pres. Arroyo mangles press freedom and carries out extra-judicial killings of human rights leaders, journalists, religious leaders and lawyers and opposition politicians with unbridled license.

Her notoriety as extremely corrupt president in Asia robs off on the Filipino people because it reveals our own propensity for corruption if given the opportunity more so

11

because political leaders from both camps are equally guilty of practicing the same venalities once they are in power.

Perhaps by exposing them to the Filipino people, these erring leaders would change their values and manner of governance. If to some extent it could be accomplished, then Dr. Mamot's efforts would be worth the undertaking.

Since being a former Political Analyst in the Office of the President, Malacanang Palace, along with his teaching of political science at Indiana University-Purdue University and University of Indianapolis (formerly Indiana Central University), he has learned to hone and sharpen his insights on the need for good government and responsible leadership.

Pres. Arroyo's corrupt government has been exacerbated by her alter egos who feel free to do the same because leadership is by example. After all they can get away with their venalities unscathed since nobody has the temerity and moral courage to expose and denounce them. Not Pres. Arroyo since she tacitly condones corruption and government anomalies particularly if those guilty officials are from her party.

Sad but true. The pains and sufferings caused by the magnitude of corruption and cruelty the military and corrupt officials, starting with the president, heap upon the nation, are real and therefore difficult to ignore or whitewash.

A host of public functionaries involved in massive corruption reads like who's who in the Arroyo government, and who are now ecstatic over their power and unexplained wealth. Corruption is unstoppable because people just fold their arms and do nothing. Putting public interest under the selfish ends of corrupt officials will not merit a salute of appreciation in Dr. Mamot's book. To him cowardice is unpardonable and inexcusable particularly when countless Filipinos are suffering from poverty.

In light of the anomalies the Arroyo government is guilty of – we are almost inclined to believe Hitler is right in saying that the "victor is never asked if he told the truth." Pres. Arroyo herself is never questioned whether her government represents integrity or why she is sitting on top of bayonets- coddled by generals to keep her in power. In turn she pampers them with juicy positions in the civilian government. One cannot ignore the fact that most key cabinet positions and other government agencies are being occupied by retired army generals.

For his courage and insightful analyses of the socio-economic malaise the hapless Filipinos are enduring under the defiled and corrupt leadership of Pres. Arroyo, we thank and doff our hat to Dr. Mamot.

Author's Note

There has been a persistent political buzz that pardoned Pres. Joseph "Erap" Estrada is reportedly eyeing on running again for the presidency in May 2010. That since such development is creating political controversy – and some excitement among the Estrada camp – it is felt that I should include here the thoughts of Jose Mari Mercader, the Executive Editor of the Filipino Times, New York City, for whatever it's worth. It appears in the Filipino Times edition of January 5-12, 2008:

Battle Of Egos

Former Pres. Fidel V. Ramos has an ego that towers Rizal monument in Luneta. He should prune it to bring him back to planet earth instead of floating up there like astral debris. His ego is pricked because talks are drumbeating the scenario of Pres. Estrada being urged by his fanatics to launch his presidential candidacy two years from now. The noise has thrown Pres. Ramos into a fit of panic, if not outright annoyance. He threatens to jump into the presidential derby if Estrada is a candidate.

What is happening to the poor old soldier, is he in his second childhood already? Just because Erap supporters are delirious to see him back, more out of sympathy that he was denied his full term, does not mean the action superstar is aggressively pursuing that delusion. In a height of egotism, Fidel challenges Erap on a one-on-one face off. It is obvious he cannot stand the idea that a mere school dropout succeeded him as president, and perhaps could have been a better chief executive had the latter finished his term.

In hindsight the Ramos presidency leaves a lot to be desired. It was so depressing anybody, even a clown, could be an enormous improvement after him. In fact it can be anticipated that the economy, peace and order, social life and foreign relations will incrementally improve without Fidel in the vicinity of the Malacanang Palace after the elections. In plain language the Philippine Republic is very much above water since he vacated the presidential office.

The hot speculation that Erap will carry the torch for the opposition in 2010, is pure conjecture – nothing tangible to it. Fidel, however, brandishes his fist hysterically shouting that he too will be available if Erap runs. In reality Fidel enthrones his ego by his maniacal display of envy. Undaunted, Estrada says he will "give Fidel plus 8 million votes ahead and still I will win by a big margin." I believe that because Erap is the favorite of the masses.

Clearly, Fidel is terrified by the prospects of Erap becoming president. Actually he is hallucinating because former Senator Franklin Drilon already doused this hyped euphoria. He says the real candidate is Senator Jinggoy Estrada whose father is crafting a Villar-Jinggoy tandem with Erap's son as vice-president. Villar has risen as the hottest would-be presidential timber in the national election two years from now (barring the CHA CHA nonsense). Although among the has-been presidents ogling to be recast as candidates in 2010, Erap is the most qualified mainly because he really did not complete his term as president while the others did the full cycle of six years. The Constitution prohibits a second term for president.

Only a political pinhead like Fidel would require blood transfusion to survive the nightmare of seeing Erap president again. Fidel's ego is implacable and he is raving like a lunatic chicken (pollo loco). Is he afraid his corrupt-ridden administration will be exhumed if Erap wins? The question may also be raised how he comes to his present fabulous wealth coming as he does from modest beginnings.

By his unrestrained abomination of Erap, the West Point graduate unwittingly displays vindictive leadership, which is unhealthy for a fledgling nation like ours, if the people are stupid enough to elect him yet. His unpalatable attitude hammers the 1st nail in the coffin of his being a nonentity out of power. All he does these days is shadow fight as if he is indispensable to our people. He expects to acquire self importance in 2010. Shakespeare already ponders on the apt question – "If to do were as easy as to know what were good to do? Fidel should be happy he is a footnote in our history, as the only president who went gallivanting around the globe on first class accommodations at government expense throughout his incumbency. His voracious appetite for junkets is unparalleled.

No doubt he is so enamored with the presidency. He can use all the funds of his office without giving an accounting to the people as he did when he was president, and still indulged in his passion of circumnavigating the world.

The reason Fidel is interested in running, which should be a caveat to the electorate, is too ugly to contemplate. We can begin with his noncompliance to give comprehensive and thorough accounting of his office huge budget when he wound up his term. Another is his failure to report where the billions of pesos of the Centennial Celebration budget went. Or better yet, who pocketed the money, how much went to him, and so on. He claims to be the country's best president. I think he misspelled beast as "best." I see no visible accomplishments worthy to merit him another tour of office in Malacanang. For the voters to give him the opportunity again would be despicable masochism. Power emanates from the governed. It would be the fault – a crying shame - of our electorate to elect a man whose sole interest in being president is to voraciously enjoy the awesome power of the office, not to uplift the nation and stabilize the economy as has been his penchant. Or he would not have sold Camp Bonifacio. Where did the money go? How much is his "commission?" According to Erap when he took over the presidency from Fidel, the legacy he got is zero budget. I believe him.

View 1

Victory Of Honasan And Trillanes: "Ridicules" The Elections

Yes, if you believe Malacanang National Security Adviser Norberto Gonzales. This is the reaction of Gonzales when he hears that Senator-elect Antonio "Sonny" Trillanes IV is ratcheting a move to "IMPEACH PRES. ARROYO" again!

Gonzales says that they are disheartened and disturbed that Trillanes is going to use his Senate position with a sole "agenda of destabilizing the Arroyo administration." He declares: "We're really dismayed about his (Trillanes) pronouncement. It's now very clear that he has no platform of government when he ran and won the Senate seat but only to destabilize the Arroyo presidency." What a way of blunting the edge of coherence.

In a rather oblique manner, Gonzales hints that the Filipinos should be castigated for electing Trillanes and Honasan since the elections are not a manifestation of the unhappiness and disgust of the Filipino the people, but it was a "ridicule vote." Just exactly what does he mean by such an infantile assumption. It is bitingly ridiculous, if I may say so myself. What a clumsy virago of a political mouthpiece of Pres. Arroyo.

Gonzales pompously declares: "We don't call it an indication that our people were mad and disgusted at President Arroyo, nor a sign that they want her out from office rather, we view it as a ridicule vote of our electoral system." Imagine the impertinence of such a statement! What a doloric kind of mentality, odious and grim.

It would be safe to say that if there is going to be a race in this Arroyo administration between the tortoise (stupidity) and hare (sanity and reason), bet on the former.

Meanwhile, the Court of Appeals debunks the petition for certiorari and prohibition filed by Marine Col. Ariel Querubin, who claims that they are not going to get a fair trial form the general court martial because Gen. Hermogenes Esperon, the Chief of Staff, is the court's convening authority, the prosecutor and the judge.

Querubin, former Scout Ranger commander, along with Brig. Gen. Danilo Lim, former Marine commandant Maj. Gen. Renato Miranda and Lt. Col. Custodio Parcon, a Medal of Valor awardee like Querubin, are being detained in a military jail. All are facing several charges before the military court, including violation of Article of War 6, or mutiny and violation of Article of War 9, or conduct unbecoming an officer and a gentlemen.

Upon hearing the CA decision, AFP-Public Information Office chief Lt. Col. Bartolome Bacarro says the decision also vindicated AFP chief Gen. Hermogenes Esperon Jr. from allegation that he is persecuting the accused. The CA decision, according to Bacarro, should clear once and for all the contentions by some quarters that are seeking to prevent the military tribunal from pushing through with the trial of the renegade officers.

The AFP spokesman declares that "It (allegation against Esperon) has been clarified in this ruling of the Court of Appeals, so it clarified everything. It clarified those issues." He further observes that the Court of Appeals has recognized that the ongoing court martial proceedings are distinct from the civil courts, It should be noted that among those being investigated are Senator-elect Honasan who is facing a coup d'etat case before a Makati City court in connection with the July 2003 Oakwood mutiny.

View 2

Pres. GMA Should Join Erap Estrada In Jail!

If one would consider the most recent report on corruption by the Transparency International (TI). This latest disturbing annual Corruption Index, ranks the Philippines in the 133rd out of 179 countries surveyed last year. Our country's index score is "2.5" with 10 being the maximum corruption-free score. The index score for Singapore and Sweden: 9.3.

Want to know our corruption index in 2001 before Pres. Arroyo grabbed power from then seating Pres. Estrada through EDSA II: RP was placed at 65th in 2001 with an index score of 2.9; 77th in 2002 with score of 2.6; 92nd in 2003 with a score of 2.5; 102nd in 2004 with a score of 2.6, 117 in 2005 with score of 2.5 and 121st last year with a 2.5 score. It is clear that since Pres. Arroyo assumed the presidency, corruption in the Philippines has been steadily increasing. Even going beyond the narrowest connotation of the word CORRUPTION, the Philippines has an unenviable record of being one of the most corrupt-ridden countries in the world under Pres. Arroyo.

If we were to give credence to the latest report, then underneath the seemingly charming smile of our lady president lies the fact that our country fares much better under the administration of then Pres. Estrada. Our Transparency International ranking was 40th place in 1997 with an index score of 305, 55th in 1998 with an index score of 3.3; 54th in 1999 with a score of 3.6.

As if putting a finishing touch to said corruption-rich scenario currently obtaining in our country is the ZTE-NBN investigation in the Senate. There are talks that Comelec Chairman Benjamin Abalos Sr is alleged to be more than neck-deep involved. Why, the name of the First Gentleman Miguel Arroyo is even mentioned; also the name of the Speaker of the House Jose De Venecia, to mention a few visible, high profile "big fish" in the Arroyo government.

Last week, it was bruited about in the media that former National Economic and Development Authority (NEDA) chief Romulo Neri would "spill the beans." Then Pres. Arroyo earlier says that Mr. Neri who has been demoted to be the head of the Commission on Higher Education would not be able to attend the Senate hearing to answer questions because she needs him in New York City during the UN 62nd General Assembly. The public reaction is swift: Pres. Arroyo is "scared as hell" that Neri would reveal the entire sordid drama of corruption in the high places that includes Malacanang. Some senators condemn the evading tactic of Pres. Arroyo: "hijacking, hijacking, hijacking." The scrappy President sensing the negative repercussion of her earlier decision orders Neri not to join her and instead remain in the Philippines to face the Senate probers. And so Mr. Neri has to stay. But what a classic example of how one high Arroyo government official does a splendid lesson in "how to toe the line." Now, Neri is belting out a different tune.

Reports from Manila had it that as of last week, the First Gentleman Mike Arroyo flies to Hong Kong after his name is linked to the ZTE-NBN corruption scandal. Remember the money involved here is not exactly peanuts: US$329 million. And Mr. Arroyo's departure is reported prior to De Venecia's revelations before the Senate hearings.

Will the First Gentleman attend the Senate hearing? Nobody knows at this stage. If he is out of the country (and he always goes out of the country every time there is a crisis involving his wife. During the time when Pres. Arroyo is about to resign, he and his congressman son left for California and did not return until it is clear that his wife is "safe."), it would be difficult to summon him. One has to consider his state of health. He underwent heart by-pass not too long ago.

Why the role of Comelec Chairman Abalos key to the Senate investigation? He is the broker between the Philippine government and Chinese ZTE NBN all along. He allegedly offers a $10-million bribe to the son of House Speaker De Venecia, whose name happens to be Jose De Venecia III, just to withdraw in the contract bidding.

Before Pres. Arroyo left for New York City to attend the 62nd UN General Assembly, she orders the "suspension of the ZTE contract." Mind you, the word here is "suspend." Not to completely scrap it! Or to punch it. So there is still a chance to revive it when things cool off.

In this week's third hearing of the Senate investigation, former NEDA administrator Neri and Comelec Chairman Abalos have to slug it out as regards the credibility issue. Neri testifies that Abalos did talk to him in three occasions. In one meeting that took place in Wack-Wack Golf Course, Abalos is reported to have offered Neri P200 million to approve the ZTE-NBN contract. Of course, Abalos flatly denies it. He denies too that he is "brokering" the ZTE deal in five or six meetings at Wack-Wack, at the Chinese Embassy dinner, at meetings with ZTE officials in Szhenzhen, China. So what in the hell is he doing in those "meetings" that took place in Manila and China all along? Incredible. It sure looks like a way of a buaya (crocodile) upon a bedrock of lying through the teeth!

Commissioner Abalos testifies that he only went to China once at the "invitation" of the Speaker's son, De Venecia III. But Sen. Jinggoy Estrada shows the Bureau of

Immigration records indicating that Abalos went to China six times between 2006 and 2007.

During the Senate hearings last week when accusations and counteraccusations are flying like hot pancake at IHOP between Neri and Abalos, Sen. Mirriam Defensor, a feisty former judge that she is, walks out but before she does, she blurts out loud: "Pinag-aawayan lang ninyo and kickback ninyo." Whoa!

Coming from Sen. Defensor, it is indicative that our country is detail-laden, sprawling nation of unchecked corruption. Want a bet? Nothing as shown before will come out of these ZTE-NBN Senate investigations. Chisel that on the Romblon marble!

View 3

Why Is AFP Flaunting The Voice Of The Filipinos?

Latest news indicates that there are incontrovertible stirrings of support of Senator-elect Antonio Trillanes by the Filipino people. More than 11 million Filipinos voted for him to be our senator. So why is Gen. Hermogenes Esperon, AFP Chief of Staff still insisting in detaining him in a marine brig? Gen. Esperon, is mentioned as one of the generals who supposedly participated in vote-rigging and cheating in May 2004 elections in favor of Pres. Arroyo. Another name is retired General Hermogenes Ebdane, now the current Secretary of National Defense. Is the AFP Chief of Staff weak-kneed and footloose in disregarding the voice of our people through honest elections? It is bruited about that he is one of the Garci generals that abetted Pres. Arroyo in vote rigging in May 2004!

Consider if you must, the act of Gen. Esperon in flauntingly snubbing the Senate probes with Executive Order (EO) #464. In one remembers, EO 464 is a gag rule imposed on all government executives by Pres. Arroyo. The Supreme Court had already declared it as "unconstitutional." So why is the AFP Chief of Staff believes that "Executive Order 464 is still in effect." EO 464 prohibits government executive as well as security officials from attending congressional investigations unless they obtain clearance from the President. In striking down the gag rule by the president, the Supreme Court rules that it is only during the "Question Hour" where permission from the President can be sought, otherwise, all those summoned by Congress must appear before it, with or without presidential nod or expressed permission.

Senator-elect Trillanes is still being detained. He announces lately that he plans to initiate a Senate investigation of the 2004 elections which implicated some the AFP generals including Gen. Esperon, who was the former AFP's deputy chief of staff for operations and he is also the head of military's Task Force Hope (Honest, Orderly and Peaceful Elections) in 2004.

In his justification to continue to detain Sen-elect Trillanes, Esperon claims:

"There are military rules to follow. This is not a fight between Senator Trillanes and the Armed Forces of the Philippines. We simply have to follow the rule of law and procedures because they are all there. Otherwise, if we do not do that, then who else could follow (military) rules and regulations?" With this rationale, Esperon continues to deprive Trillanes the people's mandate to be a member of the Senate of the Philippines. Esperon – and Pres. Arroyo – should be careful – be very careful in handling the Trillanes case. The reason is obvious: Pres. Arroyo and the military authorities appear alarmed over the information that countless officers and enlisted men in the AFP have secretly helped Trillanes. What bothers the Palace is that many officers and men have openly rejoiced Sen-elect Trillanes's victory. It has been recently reported which is confirmed and admitted by presidential legal adviser Sergio Apostol that the 3rd Infantry division, along with other officers and soldiers in other divisions remain avid and ardent supporters of Senator Trillanes.

Leery and jittery Apostol adds: "As long as these soldiers and supporters of Trillanes in the military hierarchy do not engage in destabilization acts, it (support for Trillanes) would not be a problem for us in Malacanang." He continues: "If they would only air congratulatory remarks and praises to their (former) comrade in arms, it's okay with us. There's no case against them. Anyway, we are sure they are all loyal to the chain of command."

But why would Maj. Gen. Ben Dolorfino, declare a policy that the military and the police will be forming teams that will again be deployed in metropolitan urban poor areas. The military's purpose: to create "civilian-military relations." Interestingly enough, he says that the military deployment would be in metro Manila where pockets of poverty are found. Massive demonstrations against the administration could start in Manila and Makati since both cities have mayors who are from the opposition, i.e., Mayor Alfredo Lim of Manila, and Mayor Jejomar Binay of Makati.

Deprive Trillanes of his mandate as a senator, and Pres. Arroyo and Gen. Esperon would likely find themselves in a heap of trouble at some later time. There is a groundswell of support of Trillanes. Outgoing senator to serve as Mayor of Manila Alfredo Lim observes: "any move toward denying Trillanes his senate seat might be taken negatively by the more than 11 million Filipinos who voted for him. He is certainly not a flight risk nor is he expected to be a security risk," Senator-elect Francis "Chiz" Escudero observes: "He should be allowed to perform his mandate as a senator. He should be allowed to perform his functions. There are no two ways about it. More than 11 million Filipinos said that."

Sen. Manuel "Mar" Roxas makes known his position: "Our people's choice as stated in the May 14 elections must prevail. Trillanes, by virtue of his nearly 12 million votes, should be allowed to attend all Senate functions, including our afternoon sessions. He must be permitted to serve the people and the AFP should help him, not hinder him, from performing his new mandate. If this means taking the trouble of escorting him every day to and from the Senate, then so be it. The people have spoken and we must respect their decision." On the swish of unnecessary punishment, one could display strong defiance. Like a caged animal, it could attempt to strike back sooner or later.

View 4

Say What, Madam President?

Kababayans, listen and listen good. The most outlandish statement of Pres. Arroyo in the State of the Nation (SONA) on July 23: "My target is to put the Philippines in the ranks of First World nations in 20 years." Say that again? I thought she has only three years to be president to end in May 2010. Is she planning to stay for twenty years more! Her rah-rah boys say: "Why not, she is young, vivacious and pretty!" Nandoon na ako (ok, agreed). But that is a scary prospect for our country, our people. Not too long ago, she urges presidential wannabes "not to be impatient; wait till 2010." Translated: "I will step down when my term is over." Don't count on it. Pres. Arroyo is known to change her mind more times than one mechanic rotates old worn-out tires!

Does she lack the moral weight to sink herself deep into such level of impertinence, if not utter lie. Remember, when she is campaigning during the 2004 presidential elections? She promises then: "I will solve corruption. That would be my priority." Then in a more loquacious manner she says that she will solve communist insurgency in one year! By golly, when will her lying to high heavens cease? Either she is dense and irresponsible or insulting the intelligence of the Filipinos.

Just exactly how will she do it taking for granted that she will stay around for 20 years in Malacanang. Woe to the Filipino people if that happens! For a president with a Ph.D.

in economics it is amazing that she does not seem to know that for every P1-tax that her government has been collecting during her incumbency, 93 centavos go to service our national debt!

University of the Philippines economist Benjamin Diokno observes that except for 2004, the Arroyo administration has consistently failed to meet its own gross domestic product (GDP) growth rate targets, which is normally used as basis in tracking economic growth. He continues: "The gap between the promise and actual performance has been widening and it would be much wider if no further reforms are adopted. Given how weak the government is, however, further reforms are highly unlikely." Given this economic reality, Pres. Arroyo SONA promise is an empty bombast. Another exultant statement of utter falsehood.

On March 27, 2007, the Asian Development Bank's (ADB) Asian Development Outlook 2007, released a report indicating that the Philippine economy has been showing some moderate progress which is "not enough to address the country's worsening problems of unemployment, under-employment, and poverty," Diokno adds.

Political nonsense seemed to have outgunned reason in this Arroyo administration. Consider the fact that:

1. When Pres. Arroyo assumed power in 2001, the national government's outstanding debt was P1.9 trillion; it is now P3.9 trillion. Meaning: a P2 trillion increase.
2. The P854.4 billion spent to service the national government's debt, covering interest and principal, 2006 is almost equal to what it collected in taxes of P860 billion during the year.
3. For every 100 pesos collected in taxes, P99.35 went to debt servicing.

4. Based on World Economic Forum, the Philippines' ranking in global competitiveness has been failing, from ranking of 48 in 2000 to 71 in 2006.

5. Philippine's investment is "extraordinary low at about 15 percent," as underscored by Joachim Von Amsberg, World Bank's country representative, at the Philippine Development Forum held in Cebu on March 8 and 9.

6. Not enough jobs were created, inflation remained high, and consequently the 2006 misery index is higher than the 2000 level.

During the SONA speech, Pres. Arroyo laid the groundwork with a plan "to spend P1.7 trillion on infrastructure in the next three years." To which former Pres. Fidel Ramos (the "urong sulong" president) characterizes as "all promises." He says that these promises are no different to her previous SONA speeches. This week policy speech is an "old tune."

Sen. Francis Escudero says that Pres. Arroyo seems to be unmindful of the true state of the nation, i.e., people are suffering and going to sleep hungry. She gingerly dismisses the many polls indicating that the Filipino people do not trust her. To which she counters: "I better be right than popular." Madam you are not popular because they don't trust you." Reason: They know that you cheated in May 2004 presidential elections to remain in power.

However, as usual her followers and supporters in Congress offers laudatory comments. Northern Samar congressman Raul Daza praises Pres. Arroyo. He says the "presentation was very comprehensive. It covers Luzon, Visayas and Mindanao. We hope this will promote economic growth in the countryside."

House Minority Leader San Juan Rep. Ronaldo Zamora declares that Pres. Arroyo's SONA fails to mention the extra-judicial slayings and murders of opposition leaders and civil rights groups. To squash dissent, she uses the military and police to brutalize the populace.

Pres. Arroyo mentions the political ambitions of her opponents. She intones: "I repeat. I will not be a hindrance to anyone who has political ambitions. But make no mistake. I will not stand idly (by) when any one gets in the way of the national interest and tries to block the national vision. From where I sit, I can tell you, a President is always as strong as she wants to be."

Big promises, Madam President. Your vision is like cracked mud in the parched and dried up riverbed of Pampanga River.

View 5

RP Is A Corrupt Nation For Nothing

Imagine if you must, that you are nominated for a cabinet position by Pres Arroyo that requires confirmation by the Commission on Appointments. If you were ready to put a finishing touch to the presidential appointment, or if you think that it is a slam dunk certainty that you will be a cabinet member, think again. Throw that assumption to the winds.

It is revealed by no less than our Speaker of the House, Jose de Venecia, who is alleging that extortion money is being asked by some members of the Commission on Appointments (CA) for the needed confirmation. If you think that it is a farcical production of a malicious mind, think again.

You will recall that Domingo Panganiban, chairman of the National Anti-Poverty Commission, alleges that some members of the CA had approached him and tried to exact money from him in exchange for his confirmation as then secretary of the Department of Agriculture. Now, Sen. Lacson is demanding that Panganiban come out with names who are involved in the CA "fleecing" and "blatant extortion." The Cavite senator says: "I think in due time they will have to name names because they started accusing some members of the CA particularly members of the House of the Representatives." He is not only referring to Panganiban but also Finance Secretary Margarito Teves and his father, Negros Occidental Rep. Herminio Teves, who brought out the alleged CA extortion scheme.

It is hoped that such allegations would bring into orbit of possible investigation. If it is true, then it would provide a portrait of congressional decay or freezer burn.

Who could be the legislators-of-the-moment involved in this disturbing corruption? If you ask Senator Miriam Defensor Santiago, there is nothing that could come out of any investigation. She doubts if something revelatory would ensue from such inquiry into the "racket." Sen. Santiago claims: "Extortion, like bribery, takes place only between two people, and one of them has to testify for the charge to stick. Generally, no nominee will incriminate himself by testifying that he obtained confirmation by giving a bribe, an appointment or a contract to a CA member." That statement serves as more than a classic coy snippets of Philippine politics. So with that frame of mind, let bribery in the CA go its own merry way. Lamentable. What a total-immersion corruption in the congressional corridors of power.

What is a Commission on Appointments (CA)? It is an independent government body. It is composed of 24 members, i.e., 12 from the House of Representatives and 12 from the Senate. It can promulgate new rules and guidelines insofar as its administration and operation.

Sen. Lacson in the light of these allegations, proposes that CA members would be barred from speaking to any Cabinet nominee. As it stands now, Sen. Lacson reveals that "unethical as it is, there are no existing rules barring that. The act of seven (members of the CA) talking to a nominee should be made punishable." He mentions particularly the amendment that now prohibits CA members from invoking Section 20 of the body's rules on the last day of the Congress' session or before it goes on sine die adjournment.

This time. Sen. Santiago is backing up the idea of Sen. Lacson. To avoid further erosion of the trust of the people in

CA, Sen. Santiago demands that there should be a needed change. She cites: "Under the notorious Section 20, it takes only one CA member to veto all the rest of the 23 other members. This one-person veto is what empowers a CA member to extort bribes, government appointments or public works contract in exchange for confirmation."

Viewed in this light, one could then assume that our current Philippine Permanent Representative to the United States Ambassador Hilario Davide did not bride any CA member since he did not receive the official confirmation from assuming his current position.

What is Pres. Arroyo's reaction to the CA scandal? Press Secretary and presidential spokesman Bunye states that Pres. Arroyo should not be "dragged into the issue." But she is our president and this is happening under her watch! Do we have to beatify with some touch of nostalgia the many such statements in the past from Malacanang? Madame President, you are the President. Your own nominee is being burned by corrupt CA member(s) and you just sulk in some kind of splendid isolation in Malacanang Palace by saying "I don't want to be dragged into the issue" No wonder all your senatorial candidates lost in May. People have lost all the cathode ray of hope in your leadership.

View 6

The Hunt Of Marine Killers Goes On!

The Armed Forces of the Philippines (AFP) has dispatched 500 Philippine Marines along with 300 additional PNP troops to Basilan to hunt down the MILF rebels who killed 14 Marines, 10 of whom were decapitated and mutilated in a July 10 vicious ambush in Basilan, Mindanao.

The target of the government military operations is focused on some remote villages in Al-Barka. There is one interesting aspect in this military raid: The MILF is supposed to have been served with a "warrant of arrest" before the onslaught. If the government is hell-bent on running after the Muslim culprits guilty of beheading the Marines, why would they be served first with "warrants of arrest" before the military would engaged in a retaliatory campaign?

According to Sr. Supt. Salik Macapantar of the Basilan Police Provincial Office director: "We knocked on three houses but there was nobody there. We also went to a suspected MILF camp nearby but it was abandoned as well." But, of course, common sense dictates that if you are to launch a military offensive against the enemy, you don't have to issue public statements that you are going to launch a counter-offensive military operations. It is pretty dumb, if I may say so myself.

In the political arena, Basilan Rep. Wahab Akbar appeals to the government that instead of conducting military operations against those who decapitated the 14 Marines, the Arroyo administration should instead focus on socio-economic solutions to the Muslim festering problems in Mindanao.

In a privilege speech, Akbar says that had the AFP leadership coordinated with the local officials who appraised them on the actual situation in the area, "the unfortunate massacre of the 14 Marines could have been prevented."

Rep. Akbar underscores that it is poverty and human rights abuses that create armed resistance. Instead of spending "billions and billions of pesos for military personnel, logistics and ammunitions to kill Filipino Muslim rebels, the money should instead be used for development and education." It makes sense. What a clenched fistful of reasons!

In another front, not military but on economy, the World Bank (WB) suggests to the Arroyo administration last week: "make better use of aid funds." Perhaps due to the concern by WB over the inability of the Arroyo government to make good use of international aid package, just 15.2 percent of the total aid pledged by the WB had been disbursed so far. This is slower than in the previous year and below the 20-percent agreed target.

It was recently revealed that the actual amounts released in 2007 and 2006 both stood at around $137.2 million, compared to the pledged amounts of $410 million and $395 million. WB money, like a caged lion, does not want to be held by the tail. The world financial organization knows that corruption in the Philippines is widespread and endemic.

Why this reduced aid of monetary aid by the WB to the Philippines? The WB justifies it: "The slow disbursements is attributed mainly to issues linked to insufficient level of readiness, complex project design, slow progress in policy reforms on which the release of loans is hinged, and delays in budget approval and/or release by the government."

This bottleneck in releasing WB pledged aid is unfortunate since the money was supposed to improve the school construction program which would benefit the Filipino children. WB country directed Mayse Gautier met with Pres. Arroyo and he urges her to use "efficient modes of school construction" so they are "finished on time at reasonable cost and without any reported anomalies." Considering the culture of corruption in our government, WB executive Gautier might as well belt the ballad/song: "The Impossible Dream!"

View 7

Even A Tree Surgeon Can't Cut Gloria's Tree Of Lies

Yes. Before the May 14 election, as in all previous elections, Pres. Arroyo gleefully comes up with impressive graphs and charts indicating that we are indeed on our road to economic recovery. She brags that both Bureau of Internal Revenue and Bureau of Customs are successful in their tax collection efforts. On target! She glibly stammers out that the Philippine economic health is "robust."

The Philippines under her economic stewardship is "now able to pay on time our foreign debt." Woo hoo! That our peso is getting stronger compared to U.S. currency. But wait, it was learned later that peso "strength" was not due to economic upswing but primarily due to "currency speculators!" This disturbing piece of information was revealed by no less than our Central Bank governor. If you are aware of stock manipulation in Wall Street, a speculator essentially engages in "pump and dump" scheme. Meaning: pump the value of peso (yesterday was at P45.28 to a US dollar) by making it "stronger" in the market and then dump the value (meaning keep it to P49 or P50) and SELL! What a windfall profit through speculation. It is not due to our economic recovery. Even a moron knows this.

Then the Bureau of Custom and Bureau of Internal Revenue suddenly become crestfallen last week. The government had to sell government assets in several private corporations to offset the tax collection lag. This week the Secretary of Energy is sacked due to his inability to carry out the privatization policy of the Arroyo government. The budgetary crimp must be hurting.

Jefferson once said that "nothing is bothersome that we do willingly." Therefore, don't expect any "mea culpa" statement (like in the "Hello, Garci" wiretap controversy) from Pres. Arroyo. Like saying I made a "misjudgment" again!" Where is the flow of reason in this Arroyo administration? So the linchpin of economic recovery before the May 14 elections was a lie! A fabrication of a seedy mind.

Incidentally, the decapitation and mutilation of the Marine troopers in Jolo is causing a lot of headache to Pres. Arroyo. How is she handling the crisis? Will she order an "all-out war" on the MILF who admitted that its followers were responsible for such atrocities.

Follow me, if you must. A president is the Commander-in-Chief according to our Constitution. So why is she leaving the decision to AFP Chief of Staff Gen. Hermogenes Esperon whether to declare an "all-out war" or not! If the "full-scale" war against the MILF insurgents is being left on the decision of the military, there got to be something uneasy and unsettling about it. Is she abdicating the power of the Commander-in-chief to stamp out insurgency to the military? Is she lacking now the cocksure authority to quash any internal enemies?

Is she not only always inclined to be duplicitous, but now displaying leadership role in the edge of presidential inaction?

There is another disquieting aspect of the marine massacres in Jolo. Because of the government is so corrupt, i.e., spending money left and right during the campaign, there are actually not enough military appropriations so that our soldiers will have enough and functional war materiel to stage a "full-scale" war against the Muslim rebels. It was reported that both Malacanang and Camp Aguinaldo are allegedly unable to provide support to the wounded and beleaguered marine troops. No air (helicopter) support was given. No adequate ammunitions and other firepower are deployed in the area to prevent the carnage. This Arroyo government is reportedly not even able to respond to calls from wounded and dying soldiers who were outfought and outflanked by the enemies.

No wonder detained Marine Colonel Ariel Querubin, a Medal of Valor recipient and his imprisoned fellow officers shaved their heads to protest the inaction of the Arroyo government. Does the action of Col. Querubin represent only the tip of the shaved head of possible restiveness in the military?

View 8

Some Catholic Bishops Demanding Gloria's Resignation

Immediately after the Makati Glorietta 2 bombing in which 9 were killed and more than 110 were wounded, some members of the Catholic Bishops Conference of the Philippines (CBCP) sound the alarm calling for the resignation of Pres. Arroyo. Some key Catholic bishops have expressed the suspicion that the bombing is a diversionary strategy of Malacanang Palace amid the mounting call for her stepping down due to series of corruptions stalking his government. After all, the Philippines is racked with political extra-judicial murders of her critics.

There is now the latest twist to the bombing. While the Ayala Development Conglomerate, which owns Glorietta, insists that a "bomb" or "bombs" were the reason for the explosion that killed eleven people, the military reports that there were no telltale of bomb fragments or residues. That it could have been due to explosion of the septic tank housed in the basement floor of the mall.

The Glorietta 2 tragic incident has only added fresh demand that Madam Arroyo must make an exit. On October 21, CBCP public affairs chairman Caloocan City Bishop Deogracias Iniguez Jr. announces that the Catholic conference could either call a special meeting to take up the issue, or discuss it during its forthcoming general assembly.

Due to a litany of scandals in which Malacanang Palace had been implicated lately, i.e., ZTE National Broadband scandal, Cyber Education project questionable contract, among others, which involve thousands of millions of government kickbacks, Caloocan City Bishop Deogracias Iniguez Jr; Quezon City Bishop Antonio Tobias and Infanta town, Quezon province Bishop Emeritus Julio Labayen demand Pres. Arroyo must step down. Their reason is that the Lady President has lost her moral authority. That such resignation at this time would prevent a "total collapse of the government." That for her to continue to stay in power would lead only to "national chaos."

The three bishops issue a unanimous conclusion on October 20, in Quezon City ecumenical meeting: "If a regime is morally bankrupt, has propensity for falsehoods and repeatedly lies with impunity, there is no other alternative for the people but to demand that the leader, the Chief Executive, Commander-in-Chief, the President step down and resign." They continue: "It is time for the sovereign Filipino people whom she has betrayed to now speak up as one voice and resoundingly ask her to step down."

To which Pres. Arroyo on November 1, 2007 gives this message to those critics who have book-length sermon of resignation: "Let us not be distracted by the impatient few who believe that they are above the rule of law and thus are entitled to undermine the sacrifices and hard work of our people." And she shamelessly points out the latest demo-cratic exercise of our kababayans last week: "The successful outcome of our barangay and SK elections underscores the people's firm commitment to democracy and strong political institutions. That message should not be ignored by groups who are out to destroy the gains of a strong economy through extra-constitutional means." Her preoffered advice to her political detractors: "Wait till 2010 when I will step down." Really?

In the meanwhile, Young Enlisted Soldiers Active and Retired Military Police for Solidarity (Yes Arms) spokesman Ismael Aparri appeals to the CBCP leadership to come out with a clear position on the resignation. This demand has assumed some degree of urgency particularly after former Catholic priest and now Pampanga Gov. Eduardo Among "Ed" Panlillo has revealed that he receives P500,000 cash after attending a meeting called by the President in Malacanang Palace on October 11, 2007.

It would not be a surprise if any time soon, Pres. Arroyo would invite the CBCP leaders and members to Malacanang to be wooed, dined and to break one's fast, so to speak. Many suffering Filipinos perceive the Catholic bishops as a passive group willing to look the other way every time Pres. Arroyo commits government transgressions. This perception by the people has led to loss of many faithfuls, "not to mention the church leaders' loss of moral influence over their flock." Their view of the Church is laden with muted distrust. Is the Church listed in the cash register of the Palace?

Because of the past tendencies of the CBCP, some concerned Catholic adherents and followers have shown cynicism, even suspicion, that the leadership of CBCP is in actuality in cahoots with the Arroyo administration. That despite the blatant disregard of the rule of decency in public service by Pres. Arroyo, the Catholic bishops remain yielding and their "quietistic," and their que-sera-sera attitude is at best engrained – therefore, disturbing. Is this a somatological evidence of the co-existence between men of God and Lady of the morally vulgar and corrupt Palace?

Will the dining, wooing and wining days in Malacanang of the Catholic bishops over? Will the sweet smell of

Malacanang "donation" to the bishops in the past come to pass this time?

Where is the CBCP when ten top cabinet members of Pres. Arroyo resigned in disgust because of massive government irregularities and the "Hello, Garci" wiretap caper? The beleaguered Filipino people look to the Catholic bishops for moral strength and support in their demand for Pres. Arroyo to resign. But they are sorely disappointed. What is disquieting is the CBCP's call for the people "NOT" to go to streets to air their frustration and sense of government perfidy and treachery!

This time, however, there appears to be new ray of hope. After the Glorietta 2 bombing along with the recent government anomalies, some Catholic leaders have voiced concern which the Filipino people hope would result in CBCP issuing a nationwide pastoral letter calling for the resignation of Pres. Arroyo. Or would it be another occasion when their hope would be dashed away again? Another shadowy piece of contemporary past of Church's betrayal passing through in a flash?

View 9

ARRM Vote Rigging Exposed

More than the disturbing post-election developments in Mindanao, it is now clear that Pres. Arroyo "cheated" in 2004. While the evidence of the massive electoral frauds in Lanao and other Muslim provinces in Mindanao are being kept under wrap in one of the seven boxes of evidence which could have been used for her impeachment, the latest ARMM electoral cheatings would prove the content of the "Hello, Garci" wiretap. Pres. GMA cheated. No wonder she steadfastly and stoutly refuses to entertain the impeachment complaints in the House of Representatives.

The same Comelec officials and the same machinery oiled to cheat again in May 14 election are being exposed. And the picture is getting uglier as day goes by; as latest findings and developments unfold, Anyone who relishes the never-ending minutiae of election fraud revelation, he just has to read the unfolding news.

Sen. Lacson, the winning re-electionist senator, demands the resignation of Commission on Elections Commissioner Rene Sarmiento, denouncing that the poll official should make good his promise that he would resign as commissioner if what he did, i.e., have his Comelec officers get the blank election documents from the office of the treasurer and cart them off to the Maria Cristina Hotel in Iligan City, proved to be illegal. It is a practice, which serves as a re-enactment of the 2004 massive cheating in

Lanao provinces resulting in "more than one million vote margin" for Pres. Arroyo as mentioned in the "Hello, Garci" tape! A strange coincidence?

Sen. Lacson accuses Sarmiento of election irregularities. The Imus senator says: "Commissioner Samiento...clearly violated the law. He cannot, by himself, order the custodial transfer of the ERs from provincial treasurer to any Comelecc officer – especially those Garci boys (referring to Renault Macarambon who was identified as one of then poll commissioner Virgilio Garcillano's poll fraud operators in Mindanao region in the 2004 presidential elections) and then brought to a hotel." Sen. Lacson continues: "I used to hold Commissioner Sarmieto in high esteem until I saw him standing up for Comelec officials in Lanao, who clearly violated the rules of the Comelec. That's a clear violation and for a commissioner was right there – a violation was being committed right under his nose and he even had a gall to stand for these erring Comelec officials."

TV reporter Ricky Carandang of the ABS-CBN aired last May 26 the sordid drama of vote rigging done in the open. TV cameras showed Sarmiento and his election officer denying that the blank ERs for some 13 towns were brought to the Iligan hotel. Carandang follows this video take of the ERs being brought inside the hotel elevator. But Sarmiento claims he had ordered on Sunday, the custodial transfer of the ERs to Comelec officers who he says he vouches for.

The main actor here is a Comelec official in Lanao, and Garci operator in 2004. His name is Renault Macarambon. It is found out that Macarambon took the blank ERs to a hotel in Iligan City on Saturday, May 26. But on his own admission, Sarmiento claims that he officially orders the "transfer of the boxes of empty ERs" on Sunday, May 27, or a day after Macarambon takes the election documents to a hotel in Iligan City.

Sarmiento strenuously denies first the irregularity, but when confronted with the video tape, he is caught by surprise.

Guess what happens later? Sarmiento refuses to return to Mindanao as the Comelec commissioner to oversee the ARRM special elections scheduled to be held in some towns. His reason for not wanting to return to Mindanao is due to "personal health." If you believe that, then you believe that Imelda just bought the whole town of Marikina where fake Gucci shoes are supposedly manufactured. It is a falsity of a naked kind.

Jejomar Binay, the newly re-elected Mayor of Makati City, has the following statement: "Based on the little I know of Rene Sarmiento, we were part of MABINI. What he said about resigning is a serious call, especially as he himself witnesses what is happening in the hotel and the transfer of the ERs, which is very, very grave,"

Sen. Pimentel adds his observation on the matter: "Sarmento's resignation as head of Task Force Maguindanao proves the blatancy of the cheating perpetuated by the administration at the expense of clean and honest elections." With officials like them, many opposition leaders, the Commission on Elections would be racked with a legacy of a never-ending reign of cheating on behalf of Pres. Arroyo.

Sarmiento tenders his resignation on May 28 as head of Task Force Maguindanao, citing heath reasons. "If only I am physically able, I could have proceeded to Magindanao to start the investigation, but I am not Superman to be able to do that." Yeah, right! Many opposition politicians are demanding that he should resign as Comelec Commissioner, period. That includes Comelec Commissioner Benjamin Abalos, Jr.

If you think the video tape of the ABS-CBN is serious and damaging enough, wait until you learn that on May 30, several poll inspectors and watchers in Lanao and

Maguindanao arrive in Manila and claim that armed men forced them not to discharge their duties. And they cart away all the election documents along with empty ERs boxes. Also, some teachers in several places in the ARRM regions claim that they are instructed to write the names of all TU candidates in the ballot without any GO candidates' names. No wonder in many areas in ARRM, the returns indicate 12-0 in favor of TU. Himala ni Sultan Kurakot! Thumb marks used are those of children, and if they are not readily available, cats' prints, it is reported, are used. In ARMM, the results: TU 12, GO zero. And Chavit Singzon is number one! Now figure it out! As more electoral dagdag-bawas (vote shavings) reports are being spelled out in public view, let us expect some hefty charges of election deceit and trickery would be painted in bold relief. We hope the culprits be punished according to law.

View 10

Corruption 2007: So What Else Is New?

Now hear this. The latest report of April 10, 2007 of the National Trade Estimate (NTE) of the United States Trade Representatives (TR) indicates that the Philippines remains "pervasive" that serves as trade barrier. The NTE report is submitted annually to the United States Congress.

Another latest economic report issued by the Hong Kong-based Political and Economic Risk Consultancy (PERC) rates the Philippines as "the most corrupt country in Asia." It is now clear that the economic horizons in our country under Pres. Arroyo's watch are being shrouded by darkening clouds. What a worse time for these economic findings to come. In a month's time, our mid-elections will take place. I urged our fellow OFWs who are registered earlier in our New York City Consulate to cast their votes.

The seeds of accusation of widespread corruption in the Arroyo government apparently are plentiful as ever. Vote rigging is carried to the max! The latest depressing reports indicate that in terms of pervasiveness of corruption, the Arroyo government's record is even worse than during the Estrada administration.

The recent US agency says the Philippines' score in Transparency International's Annual Corruption Perceptions Index survey has averaged 2.5 to 2.6, out of a best score of 10, since 2002, which is "down from 3.6 in 1999" during the incumbency of now detained Pres. Estrada.

There are several contributory factors why corruption under the Arroyo government is considered "pervasive." One of them is due to the concerns expressed by foreign and domestic investors in our country that local courts and regulators have the propensity to "stray beyond matters of legal interpretation in policymaking functions and about the lack of transparency" in these decision-making institutions.

There is also a widespread impression among investors in the Philippines that courts are influenced by bribery and are issuing improper temporary restraining orders which serve to obstruct or impede the conduct of legitimate commerce.

The Arroyo governance is accused of being in the thick of the rush to appoint regulators who do not possess any qualifications. Investors also expressed concerns over the fact that in many instances, "business regulators lack any background in economics, or a competitive economic system and regulatory process, whether by bribery or through exploiting the lack of expertise among regulators, to protect market positions."

The Arroyo government has been trying to curb corruption by issuing executive order creating an anti-corruption watchdog known as the Revenue Integrity Protection Service (RIPS) in the Department of Finance that has worked closely with the Ombudsman to assist in reining in corruption in revenue collection agencies. But the records of the Ombudsman are woefully unimpressive so far. It has been noted that the Office of the Ombudsman has "sat on corruption cases filed against Arroyo officials and allies" The report cites the cases of former Justice Secretary Hernando Perez and former Agriculture Undersecretary Jocelyn "Joc-Joc" Bolante. Both are accused by the Senate and other private parties of diverting some P3 billion in public funds into the campaign kitty of Pres Arroyo during the presidential elections in 2004.

The Philippines has been experiencing a free fall in the international surveys lately. PERC's recent survey of businessmen tags the Philippines under Pres. Arroyo as the "most corrupt" economy in Asia, with our country falling to a 9.4 grade from a 7.8 rating in 2006, on a scale of zero to 10, zero being the best possible score. A more alarming piece of economic fact is that Philippines is just shy by .6 to earn a 10, the worst possible score! It appears that our country is caught in the surging sweep of unchecked corruption.

With economic reports like these, how can we Filipinos – both at home and abroad - experience a flash of real good feeling about this Arroyo government?

View 11

Ferdinand Lintuan: A Requiem

The festive mood of Christmas eve is wafting in the celebratory air awaiting the birth of Christ. Residents of Davao City were rejoicing in anticipation of attending mid night mass. Along the veins of exultation came two men riding in a motorcycle following a green Volkswagen. A single shot is heard. Inside the car is radio anchor Ferdinand "Batman" Lintuan along with two fellow journalists Louie Ceniza and Edgar Banzon. Obviously the target is Ferdinand 'Batman" Lintuan, who is doing a running expose on corruption in the Davao City. The bullet hits Lintuan. He succumbs instantly.

Now the glossy eyes of suspicion are turned on Mayor Rodolfo Duterte whose administration is being alleged as harboring and allowing "death squad" in the city. Some assert that these are political ninjas of the South ready and able to salvage those who criticize his administration. To his political critics his style of leadership is more than tip-of-the-tongue phenomenon of silencing his political detractors through a band of thugs known as the "death squad." To those who speak ill of him, they suffer the unspoken expectancy of possible liquidation. It is a reminiscent of Agentina and Brazil in the 1970s and 1980s.

Naturally, Mayor Duterte vehemently denies these accusations. In a ringing political prose, he declares that "there is no death squad" operating in his city. That his

54

nemesis are acting in an unrighteous indignation. No basis for their unkind cut of his leadership. Because politics is always politics no matter how one looks at it, there will always be critics. One of the bitterest political opponent of Mayor Duterte is the Davao City Congressman Prospero Nograles. He lambasts Davao Philippine National Police (PNP) which quickly announces that "there is no death squad in Davao City." He criticizes PNP Region 11 spokesman Chief Insp. Querubin Manalang when he denies the existence of the much dreaded Davao death squad. Nograles says that it is a common knowledge of the death squad's existence. He continues that denying its existence is "strange" since everybody knows that many killings in Davao City could be attributed to death squad. Salvaging of journalists is an open secret. Some members of these death squads are alleged to be police and military personnel. What a retributive justice! Vigilantism in action.

Even the UN special rapporteur Philip Alston specifically underscores the extra-judicial slayings that take place throughout the Philippines under the watch of Pres. Arroyo. The Philippine National Police spokesman argues that the existence of death squad in Davao City is a "mere speculation." The killings could be due to gangsterism. That many of the unaccounted and unsolved murders are "just among local gangs."

Nograles says that "whether it's the Davao death squad or not, there are vigilantes openly and publicly killing people in broad daylight in Davao City with no arrests and solutions by our police." The vexing question he asks: "Why?"

Lintuan has joined his fellow journalists who have been murdered in 2007.

On February 19 Hernani Pastolero, Sr., editor-in-chief of the Lightning Courier, in Cotabato City, was gunned down by a lone gunman who shot him twice in the back of his head in Sultan Kudarat, Shariff Kabunsuan while having coffee outside his home. Dodie Nunez, a freelance photojournalist for several local newspapers, was ambushed on May 21, while on his way home to General Mariano Alvarez, Cavite.

On April 18, Carmelo Palacios, a reporter for the Radyo ng Bayan, was killed in Sta. Rosa, Nueva Ecija. Another Radyo ng Bayan reporter Vicente Sumalpong was assassinated in Bongao, Tawi-Tawi. All these slayings remain unsolved.

To prove that the Philippine National Police is determined in apprehending the assassins of Lintuan, it is offering a Pl-million reward for the apprehension of the shooters. Duterte for his part is offering P500,000 bounty. Nograles has offered also a P500,000 reward for the information and apprehension of the guilty murderers.

In many parts of the country, ambushing, shooting, killing members of the media seem to be taking place with impunity because the national police is in state of denial. One does not have to be brain surgeon to be a realist and keen observer, out-of-the-box observers that in many instances, the leaders and members of these death squads are actually members and former members of the military.

How lucky we are in the United States. We can express our opinions and views without fear that we could be arrested and even murdered.

View 12

Will The New Defense Secretary Stand Up, Please!

Gilbert Cojuangco Teodoro becomes the new secretary of national defense. If he is to leave a real imprint in the defense department, he would have to be aggressive in finding the true state of our military establishment. Young officers who unsuccessfully try to overthrow Pres. Arroyo claim that the national defense department depicts a map of corruption and abuse of authority.

There is one advice, unsolicited if I may say, from a well-respected former military officer, Gen. Ramon Farolan (ret) to Sec. Teodoro. "Retire Armed Forces of the Philippines (AFP) Chief of Staff Hermogenes Esperon Jr., Marine commandant Maj. Gen. Nelson Aliaga and Western Command chief Lt. Gen. Eugene Cedo." Their collective guilt: negligence, incompetence and command responsibility for the ambush of 14 Marines, ten of whom were decapitated, along with the wounding of nine others in Al-Barka, Basilan in July 2007.

Since then, the AFP has not conducted a counter offensive to catch those guilty MILF rebels. As a matter of fact, the spokesman of the Moro Islamic Liberation Front (MILF) issues virtually a litany of brazenly pumped challenges to the AFP. "Come and get us." The MILF says that it will not identify much less surrender the killers of the Marines.

Our AFP should learn from history. Spain for more than three hundred years; and the United States for nearly fifty years never really "conquered" the Muslim provinces in Mindanao. What both Spain and United States did was merely allowed the Muslim Filipinos lived in their own territories and ancestral enclaves peacefully provided they are left alone by the white colonizers. In the end, both Spain and the United States left without completely "defeating" the Muslim Filipinos. The same thing is happening now. The MILF declares that the Marines enter its area of jurisdiction without prior notice.

So far, no arrests have taken place.

In the wake of the Basilan Marine massacre, it came to the knowledge of our people that those unfortunate troopers had "to borrow a truck" to carry out the tragic raid in Al-Barka. What a shame. Is the AFP in short supplies of military trucks? Whatever happens to the P10 billion military allocation since Pres. Arroyo came to power illegally in 2001?

Teodoro should also look into the reported anomalous purchase of mortar shells and other ammunition, radio communications equipment along with the allocation and "conversion" of intelligence funds. Remember the massive corruption case of former AFP Comptroller, ousted General Carlos Garcia. His wife, a nurse from Ohio, bought a pricey condo in eastside Manhattan, New York City. The scandal came to the public notice when two of former Gen. Garcia's sons were caught in the US airport with $100,000 in cash each.

Now we know that there is enough money, bunch of funds to steal in Camp Aguinaldo since 2001. If the AFP Comptroller Carlos Garcia is found guilty as charged and now being incarcerated, how come no AFP Chiefs of Staff, former and the present, were not investigated. One would wonder why no AFP Chief of Staff has been implicated?

The Office of the military Comptroller functions directly from the Office of the Chief of Staff. Do you mean Comptroller Garcia, who serves like a "bookkeeping clerk" in the Office of the Chief of Staff could engage in massive stealing of military funds without the knowledge of the Chief of Staff? Remember the money involved is not pittance.

If there is restiveness in the military, especially among the Marines, one could understand. Imagine with generals purchasing cars for their use, and the Marines in the battlefronts had to borrow trucks to launch a military campaign, that would be pathetic. Sad. Alarming. Especially when P10 billion was allocated since 2001 for the Basilan pacification campaign.

One advice to Secretary Teodoro: Find why the morale among the Marines is in its all-time low. Call an urgent command conference with Marine generals, colonels, majors, captains, and lieutenants and even sergeants without the presence of Generals Esperon, Aliaga and Cedo. Give them an opportunity to air their grievances and gripes.

But then that would be rocking the boat. Knowing the close, very close, affinity of Pres. Arroyo with the top military leaders, Teodoro would be treading in a risky path. I doubt whether Teodoro would have the guts to heed the advice.

View 13

If It Smells Like A Suspect – Make An Arrest!

The Arroyo sense of justice is mocking the basic notion that an accused remains innocent until proven guilty. Obviously, Malacanang is not fully satisfied to have Sen. Trillanes IV and his Peninsula "coup" group in detention. As of this writing, the military and police authorities are still looking for more "suspects." The dragnet is getting wider. Under Pres. Arroyo's distorted and obstreperous semantic, "suspected" means "guilty." Hence, these "suspected" individuals should be hunted down and captured no matter what. Offer a bounty on their heads. Another disturbing linguistic distortions being subscribed to by the Arroyo repressive government. If you are an opposition politician, then ex cathedra you are "guilty" of rebellion!

Consider, if you must, the case of Makati Mayor Jejomar Binay. In an infantile summing-up of legal interpretation, Binay is deemed a "part" of the Peninsula Hotel "coup" since two of his security officers are reported or seen to be holed in the hotel at the time of the siege.

Philippine National Police chief Avelino Razon Jr. ejaculates the misplaced claim that "there are four groups" involved in the supposed failed "rebellion." But he has no evidence or proof to substantiate his claim. In the same vein, Armed Forces of the Philippines Chief of Staff Gen. Esperon Jr. also blurts out loudly that the detained officers in Tanay detention are part of the Peninsula Hotel abortive "coup." To buttress this outlandish and reckless allegation, both he and the National Police chief Razon claim that the Communist Party of the Philippines (CPP) is "linked with the plot!" That is pure buncombe. Military malarkey, at best!

Chief Razon further trumpets that when the police "captured" the "rebels" under Sen. Trillanes, documents were found indicating the blueprint of "revolutionary" government the coup plotters would adopt. What is disturbing to note is that in the six hours of being holed up in the hotel, the "plotters" could have destroyed the documents. They are not knuckleheads or pinheads just to leave the "document" scattered all around the hotel rooms for the police and military to find. Remember, most members of the Trillanes group are Philippines Military Academy graduates. When they are arranging for their "surrender," they had enough time to destroy these pieces of documentation. But they did not.

Let's go back to Mayor Binay. Veiled in the elaborate garlands of manufactured complicity, Department of Justice Secretary Raul Gonzalez orders the National Bureau of Investigation (NBI) to look into the possibility of Mayor Binay's involvement in the Peninsula standoff. Gonzalez believes that Binay, who is also the president of the United Opposition, must have a hand in the "coup." His reason: Binay's security men were seen with the Trillanes group. At least two of Binay's security detail are former Staff Sgt. Elmer Colon and Sony Madarang who are seen hanging around in the hotel premises. Sgt. Colon is reported to be wearing a wig to disguise his identity.

Mayor Binay never denies that both men are part of his city hall security detail. But he is quick to point out that their presence at the Peninsula Hotel is not known to him, or that he authorizes their presence in the hotel at the time. He adds that he did not know Sgt. Colon personally. Binay claims: "Malacanang is determined to crush the legal opposition, even if it means twisting the truth in order to arrive at a justifiable, but far from factual, ground for my suspension, and similar punitive measures against opposition leaders." Interesting added footnote: Mayor Binay's wife has an outstanding arrest warrant for complicity in a City Hall corruption during the time when she was the mayor.

The Arroyo administration is known for its propensity to send mixed signals thus confusing the public. After Gonzalez' claim of Binay possible participation, Department of Interior and Local Government Secretary and Presidential Adviser on Political Affairs Ronaldo Puno pooh-poohs Gonzalez' suspicion. Says he: "I find no strong reason to conclude that Binay has something to do with the stand off nor could he accuse the mayor of neglecting his duties while the crisis is going on." Puno continues: "It's too early to talk about that because all these things they are talking about or have been reported are all circumstantial. Just because there are these reports do not mean there is complicity. It's hard to be a local executive, if these things happen all the time, no mayor will be able to work and will spend all his time facing investigations."

As if leaping into the air of his own counterpunch, Mayor Binay urges the NBI to investigate Gen. Esperon after he admits earlier to have received "advance intelligence reports about the walkout at the Makati Court and the takeover of Manila Peninsula by the group of Trillanes and Brig. Gen. Danilo Lim."

Binay wonders that if in fact Gen. Esperon has an advance knowledge of the walk out and take over of Peninsula Hotel, why did he not act to prevent such confrontation? Binay surmises aloud whether Gen. Esperon has his own agenda. He asks: "What was his reason for not sharing the information? If he had done so, then all this could have been prevented."

Even with a borderline intelligence, Mayor Binay's pointed question certainly deserves pondering. The unsettling winds of that November 29 Peninsula standoff certainly is still reverberating in a disturbing whirlwind.

View 14

"Your Days Are Numbered"

The "Emperor" has denied sending a chilling, gravely disturbing warning to Senior State Prosecutor Emmanuel Velasco, head of the Presidential Task Force Against Media Harassment now given the task of investigating the abduction of activist Jonas Joseph Burgos, son of the late publisher of the Malaya, a hard-hitting opposition newspaper from the time of the Marcos' dictatorial regime to the present time of Pres. Arroyo's administration.

Among the military circle, the "Emperor" refers to Brig. Gen. Delfin Bangit, the head of the Intelligence Service of the Armed Forces of the Philippines (ISAFP).

The text message reads in its entirety: "Hayop ka Velasco, hindi mo kaya si Emperor. Ihahabol ka naming kay Jonas (Joseph Burgos). Bilang na ang.oras mo, magtago ka na." (Damn you, Velasco. You can't beat Emperor. You will follow Jonas's fate. Your days are numbered. Better go into hiding.).

Reports in Manila had it that the following officers and men and women allegedly had knowledge, or participated in the disappearance of Jonas: Army Technical Sergeant Jason Roxas, Air Force Corporal Maria Joana Francisco, both assigned with the MIG-15 (Military Intelligence Group 15) of the ISAFP; Army Master Sergeant Aron Arroyo, also assigned with the MIG-15; Army First Lt. Jaime Mendaro, assigned with the 56th Infantry Battalion; Army Lt. Col.

Noel Clement, formerly assigned with the 56th IB and now detailed with the Philippine Army's Escort and Security Battalion in Fort Bonifacio. Another unnamed MIG officer with "TL" initial is reported to have allegedly participated in the abduction.

Velasco says that these military officers and non-commissioned officers are tagged by an informant as having participated in the Burgos abduction. Such informant is now currently under the witness protection program of the Department of Justice.

The National Bureau of Investigation (NBI) is being accused of dragging its feet in investigating the named military personnel. Its reason: they cannot be questioned by the NBI as "there was still no evidence" of their involvement in the case. This reasoning seems a tad tenuous and shallow. Just exactly how does one investigating bureau gather evidence? Wait until said evidence starts knocking on their door! For crying out loud move! Start questioning suspects and other "individuals of interest." Unless of course, the "state of denial" mentality of the Armed Forces of Philippines is deeply embedded in its psychic.

NBI Deputy Director Reynaldo Esmeralda announces that they are already working to obtain more information regarding the vehicles supposedly used. They were reported to have the following plate numbers: WAM-155 and XBC-881. The NBI is given a ten-day deadline to submit its report based on their preliminary findings.

Gen. Bangit, who was Pres. Arroyo's former chief of the Presidential Security Group (PSG) vigorously denies that he or his ISAFP men had something to do with the Burgos abduction. Denials come too from the Philippine Air Force saying those men identified are not connected with Air Force command.

So where is Jonas? Is he dead or still alive? Malacanang Executive Secretary Eduardo Ermita is quoted to have said that Jonas "is still alive" but in a precarious health condition and needs medication. The Arroyo administration assures the public that there would be "no sacred cows" in the military. That it is time for the suspects to come out in the open and belie before the bar of public opinion the allegations of their being the culprits." Say that again. "belie before the bar of public opinion." I thought we have the courts to render judgment. As if Malacanang is dead serious about the fate of Jonas, Ermita goes further in his statement: "They have to present themselves and show whether they really are involved or not, there's no leeway. Let the military commanders make them available, that's the only way we can get to the bottom of this." Fine and dandy!

While Ermita is enjoining the military commander "make them available..." the Executive Security clears Bangit, alias the "Emperor," and absolves him of any responsibility for whatever abuses his men have committed. Talking of jumping the gun. No formal investigation has yet been conducted but Malacanang has "absolved" Bangit already of any wrongdoing or for whatever abuses his men have committed. Where and what is the meaning of command responsibility?

Faced with another international censure for tolerating abduction, and extra-judicial killings which many Filipinos – along with the international human rights groups – believe that the military is in a "state of denial" – Pres. Arroyo said before the Anti-terrorist Summit in Cagayan de Oro: "I have my deepest respect to the AFP, 99 percent of them are hardworking, love this nation and abide by the rule of law. But if they do wrong it must be stopped. No one is above the law."

I am reminded of a quote by one prominent philosopher as follows: "There be three things which are too wonderful for me; the way of an eagle in the air; the way of the serpent upon a rock; the way of a ship in the midst of the sea; and the way of man with a maid." To Madam Arroyo, it would be the way of the Commander-in-Chief with a few die-hard military generals! Particularly AFP Chief of Staff Gen. Esperon. One doubts seriously if in February 2008, Pres. Arroyo would let him go despite the compulsory retirement in the military. She is morbidly afraid that the next Chief of Staff will not be as loyal to her – hence, she could be deposed through a military coup. But if Pres. Arroyo extends the tenure of Gen. Esperon, it could trigger a sustained and steely restiveness among the top military echelon. This could mean trouble for her. Remember, if one must, what deposed Pres. Marcos did in retaining his "favorite" and "trusted" Gen. Ver and his like-minded "loyal" generals. It led to Pres. Marcos' eventual political demise.

View 15

The Bombing Of The House Of Representatives

First it was Glorietta. Then the House of Representatives!

In both these bombings, lives are lost and several innocent kababayans are wounded, some are seriously. Is our country stumbling into a new, tragic cycle of violence? All because of politics?

In the recent House of Representatives bombing, the death toll is placed at 4, with 13 wounded. One of the victims who later fatally succumbed was Rep. Wahab Akbar. Police authorities suspect that Rep. Akbar is the main target. Akbar is reported to be a former member of the Abu Sayyaf who later joins the government fold. He assists the government in its anti-terrorism campaign against the terrorists in Basilan. Malacanang reports that weeks earlier, it receives a death threat against Rep. Akbar. The Arroyo administration feels that the bombing is "not" a terrorist attack but an assassination plot specifically against Rep. Akbar.

Manila Police Chief Geary Barias informs the media: "We now have evidence of a bomb…the cellphone and pieces of nails used as shrapnel. It was further reported that the cellphone text messages, supposedly from the Abu Sayyaf Group (ASG) are circulating that claimed responsibility for the bombing. Chief Barias adds: "We are not taking that hook, line and sinker." Immediately after the blast, ASG is quick to deny the report of its involvement. Kumander North Mudalam, ASG commander in Basilan flatly denies that his group is responsible for the bombing. Contrary to the police report, the ASG has "no reason" to kill Rep. Akbar.

Cesar Padlan, a cameraman of the House of Representatives who owns one of the destroyed motorcycles is interviewed by the police. The other wrecked motorcycle's ownership is being investigated by the police. The two bicycles are usually parked along each other. The police also reports that a flea market is situated near the blast site.

Shortly after the blast, the security forces in the Batasan Complex are taken over by the elite Special Action Force (SAF) of the Armed Forces of the Philippines. In addition, the 15,000 army troops in the National Capital Region have been ordered to be on red alert. The Arroyo government is taking the bombing of the Batasan Complex seriously that aside from the Metro Manila area, military and police authorities in the Northern Luzon and Southern Tagalog regions are ordered to be on heightened alert.

Does the blast of our Batasan Pambansa portend disturbing trends that more bombings could take place in our country? It is hoped that the perpetrators of such cowardice are apprehended and be brought to justice.

The United Opposition (UNO) roundly condemns the bomb blast. It declares:

"We extend our condolences to the families of those who were killed and pray for the immediate recovery of those who were injured. Sadly, this tragic incident only serves to reinforce a perception of rising lawlessness, which could have a negative impact on international perception on the stability of the Philippines. A bomb explosion within the grounds of Congress sends the chilling message that ordinary Filipinos and government officials are equally vulnerable to lawless elements, whether in their homes, on the streets or in their place of work. We do not want to add to the confusion by speculating on the motive behind the bombing. We trust that our investigating authorities will do their work and be as thorough as possible."

U.S. Ambassador Kristie Kenney conveys to the House Speaker De Venecia the U.S. government's offer of assistance in the conduct of the investigation should Pres. Arroyo so request it.

View 16

Impeach Abalos? Another Frolicking Wishful Thinking

Not while Pres. Arroyo is still the president. She is eternally grateful to Election Commissioner Benjamin Abalos Sr. for allegedly abetting in her 2004 suppopsely "bogus" victory!

Former congressman and now Iloilo Vice Governor Suplico reveals his plan to file an impeachment case against Commissioner Abalos Sr. The charge: culpable violations of the Constitution stemming from his alleged involvement in the anomalous $329-million ZTE national broadband deal.

Vice Gov. Suplico says that his team of lawyers who has been studying the case assure him that there is a good case against Abalos. During the weekly Ayes and Nays forum in the House of Representatives, Suplico observes that there are valid grounds to charge Abalos in connection with his alleged participation in the $329-million contract that the Arroyo government entered into with the Chinese firm ZTE Corp.

Suplico says that he has already in his possession enough evidence, both documentary and testimonial, to support his move for the impeachment of Commissioner Abalos. In the meanwhile, Suplico and his lawyers are planning to petition the Supreme Court to "nullify the government contract with ZTE."

However, Minority Leader Ronaldo Zamora declares that they have yet to see the evidence and the complaint to be filed by Suplico before they could make any definite action. Rep. Zamora argues that "an impeachment case is very different from an ordinary criminal case, the former requiring fool-proof evidences....we have first to see the meat of the complaint and evaluate it before we can decide on this matter." While I do not pretend to have a crystal ball, I am certain that this Abalos impeachment brouhaha will fly into the "statusphere" of failure. Abalos will resign, but not impeached. He knows too much to be caught in a political vise in the Senate, which could involve Pres. Arroyo's reported cheating in 2004.

Sen. Lacson, on the other hand, bares earlier the ZTE corruption case. He maintains that there "is division of the crooked spoils by way of kickbacks as relayed to him by his sources." Sen. Lacson says that he already has one "eyewitness" willing to testify against. Abalos in the Senate.

It is revealed that the former National Economic Development Authority (NEDA) Chief Romulo Neri, who is demoted with his appointment as Commission on Higher Education chief, reportedly rejects a P200-million bribe offer to approve the overpriced ZTE contract. But when asked later, Neri refuses to comment on it.

Lacson euphemistically describes the supposedly involved government officials in the Commission on Elections as the "Big One" and "Little One" who benefited from the alleged overpricing. The Cavite Senator continues: "He (the alleged whistleblower) will identify them and himself once he testifies in the Senate. This is really mind-boggling which is why this issue should not be stopped. What I know is that he is ready to testify. That's what he told me when we last spoke," Lacson adds. As if titillating the curiosity of the public, Sen. Lacson adds: "In fact she is already preparing her affidavit. Did I say she?" Could the "Big One" referring to Commissioner Abalos and the "Little One" to Pres. Arroyo? Or the First Gentleman, a hulk of a man, and his diminutive wife, Pres. Arroyo?

The ZTE broadband anomaly is getting more intriguing as days go by. There are demands in the halls of Congress, i.e., in the Senate and in the House of Representatives for blood! In the House, there is one interesting twist. Speaker Jose de Venecia is in favor of canceling the ZTE contract. Right away. One perhaps could understand his motivation. His son, Jose de Venecia, III, would benefit if such ZTE contract would be cancelled. Before the broadband contract with the government is being discussed, young de Venecia's company, Amsterdam Holding, Inc. is one of the major bidders. It fails to win due to some funding issue.

Senators Lacson and Pimentel consider one disturbing aspect of the ZTE caper. The security of the Philippines is mentioned since ZTE is a Chinese corporation given the responsibility of maintaining communication system in the country, thus the security of the Philippines. They raise a question: "Why give that responsibility to a foreign corporation when the PLDT has the capability to do the job?"

Malacanang reacts to the boiling issue. Executive Secretary Eduardo Ermita in a press briefing says that "definitely I don't see what liability a President can have in this. In the first place we cannot assume there is some irregularity until such time that we find out based on what the SC and the Ombudsman say. If there's something wrong found later the least that can happen is for it not to go through. So what liability would the President have?" Ermita continues: 'The President never witnessed a signing of any contract as I said I don't even know if there's really indeed a contract that was signed." What a timeless foolhardiness to think that a US$329-million contract that involves the very national security of our country – and now the subject of possible impeachment in the House and inquiry in the Senate – and the President of our country does not know about it. It would be ludicrously unbelievable!

View 17

The Money Bag Source

Just exactly where did the bagful of cash come from? Who gives the money to Pampanga Governor Eduardo Panlilio and Bulacan Governor Joselito "Jun-Jun" Mendoza. It is learned that both along with 190 congressmen and provincial official received money on October 11, when they attended a meeting held in Malacanang presided by no less than Pres. Arroyo.

Never wanting to be accused of pussyfooting on the controversial issue, Gov. Mendoza reveals on Oct. 23 that when he receives the money in the Palace, Eastern Samar Governor Ben Evardone, League of Provinces of the Philippines (LPP) secretary-general, is present. That in fact Gov. Evardone justifies the questionable political almsgiving as a means of funding "community projects." The Bulacan governor reveals that the brown bag containing P500,000 is given to him in the presence of Department of Interior and Local Government (DILG) Undersecretary Austere Panadero. Present also is the former Agusan del Sur Governor Eddie Plaza.

Obviously the Arroyo administration never wishing to be depicted as the only pebble on the beach of escalating and never-ending corruption points the accusatory finger to House Speaker de Venecia Jr. The Presidential Anti-Graft Commission announces that it is Rey Roquero, Lakas-Christian-Muslim Democrat (CMD) executive director as the person who distributes the cash. Roquero is closely identified with Speaker De Venecia.

Malacanang Press Secretary Bunye earlier admits the cash distribution and he does not mind it as long as cash donation is spent for the good of the people. Later, he denies having said it.

"Consider it (the bagful of money) as a Christmas donation," Rep. Antonio Cuenco of Cebu comments when it becomes public knowledge. Later, of course, he says that he is "merely joking" when he makes such remark. Executive Secretary Ermita gives a facile answer when he is confronted with the issue. He says that he has nothing to say about it since he is not present when it took place.

There is a talk going around that Malacanang is seriously contemplating of suspending both Governors Panlilio and Mendoza for literally spilling the beans. The possible charge being readied against the two governors: "receiving bribe!" What a notable political nomenclature of stupidity!

There seems to be one political buzzword or truism in Malacanang under Pres. Arroyo. Lying and political loyalty cohere together in redoubling their efforts when Palace occupants have forgotten their aim to serve the people. The tendency to hoodwink the Filipinos seems to be fast becoming the caricature of Pres. Arroyo's propensity for cheating.

DILG Undersecretary Panadero did not deny his presence when the brown bags of money are distributed in Malacanang. He explains that the reason he is in Malacanang on October 11 was presumably to attend the Cabinet meeting as well as the oath-taking of the new batch of officers of the Union of Local Authorities of the Philippines (ULAP). Later, he says that DILG does not have such considerable amount of money for cash-gift distributions.

Budget Secretary Rolando Andaya categorically denies that the money came from his department since his office is not allowed to give cash out without prior official authority normally done in a proper channel. Other Pres. Arroyo's servile followers, those who usually receive money from Malacanang say that the money comes from the PAGCOR. Others claim that cash gift comes from the Intelligence Fund of the Armed Forces of the Philippines. Until now the real source remains a mystery. For one thing is sure, the hundreds of millions contained in brown bags and hand given at the Palace did not come from the personal fund of Pres. Arroyo. Unless, of course, she has enriched herself and her family in office that she can give away millions. But her family or the family of her husband is not known to be that affluent or generous. Ah, the mystery remains in the celestial height of quandary.

The cry of corruption is getting louder in the Senate. The latest cash-out scandal is stoking more feverish attacks on Pres. Arroyo. The Senate has already started to investigate the dubious "cash distribution" and they already have two very credible witnesses, i.e., Gov. Panlilio and Gov. Mendoza, of Pampanga and Bulacan, respectively.

In the meanwhile, Pres. Arroyo seems to be aware that a perfect political storm is brewing in Manila. In a recent speech in Virac, Catanduanes, Pres. Arroyo expresses her political predicament. "We are now far from the political noise in Metro Manila. (AFP Chief Gen. Esperon orders the deployment of more than 6,000 army troops and national police in Metro Manila to quell any possible massive demonstrations). Even though barangay elections arc set, there is no political rift here in Catanduanes, there are no human rights violations, no political noise...I hope these things will end so we can all do our job well."

Oh, Madam President! The scandals and corruption taking place under your watch "will end" while you are in office? It is a pure irrational political pamphleteering.

View 18

Ten Thousand Peso-"Bribe" For Victory Of Malacanang Senatorial Candidates

Re-electionist senatorial candidate Lacson has plan to file "bribery" charge against Justice Secretary Raul Gonzalez. Will it stick? Or is it more of a political shadow boxing lacking substance? Or will the Arroyo administration and its staunch supporters continue to play the lie?

Sen. Lacson charges Sec. Gonzalez of bribery and corruption of public officials. Announces the senator: "My office is readying the complaint which we are planning to file ... before the Ombudsman against Gonzalez for violation of Article 212 of the Revised Penal Code and Section 3a of the Anti-Graft and Corrupt Practices Act, or RA 30l9." Lacson bases his legal argument on the ground that the justice secretary is committing bribery and corruption when he offers Pl0,000 to his campaign leaders to insure the 12-0 victory of the Team Unity bets.

Lacson is contemplating with dogged determination of including some candidates who openly come out with blatant offer of money to their campaign people to deliver victory to them.

Ah, with the hard-hitting, bone crunching kind of a political onslaught against those who insult our democratic moorings, Sen. Lacson plans to include Gov. Luis "Chavit" Singson, one of the Team Unity bets who was caught on TV news in a video "offering P50,000 to every barrio official who can deliver the votes that would land him in the first five positions in the Senate race."

In a quick retort, Singson denies the offer. He says that he is offering 50,000 amulets to the barangays, not P50,000! That to my mind is an overwrought nonsense.

The charges against Gonzalez and Singson fall within the purview of Article 212. "When you induce or persuade or offer another public officer or official with a gift or anything else in exchange for doing something, that constitutes a violation of Section 3a of RA 3019, Lacson argues.

Lacson is also eyeing Speaker Jose de Venecia and boxer Manny "Pacmam" Pacquiao for giving out free insurance coverage to voters, along with the son of PAGCOR Chairman, Ephraim Genuino who is running for Congress in the 2nd district of Makati City.

Jaro Archbishop Angel Lagdameo, CBCP president is urging the Comelec to resolve immediately the reported vote buying where Gonzalez offered his campaign leaders in Iloilo P10,000 to insure victory of all the TU senatorial candidates. Comelec Commissioner Rene Sarmiento says that the commission is now investigating the matter.

Henrietta De Villa PPCV National Chairman, comments on Gonzalez's offering: "It is unfortunate, coming from a high official in the land, the secretary of Justice, no less, that these things should be said by him. We appeal to all the candidates and officials of our country, please be careful of what you say. Even if they say it is only a joke, people will interpret it differently."

On his charge against Justice Secretary Gonzalez he files with the Ombudsman, Sen. Lacson offers the following statement: "I'd like to test the mettle of the Ombudsman because there is a new Ombudsman in the person of Merceditas Gutierrez. I am also treating this as a test case to also find out what she is going to do with this case that is very glaring and blatant since the commission of the crime was done by very openly."

Gonzalez on his part argues that what he is doing in offering money is not against the law since "I am not a candidate." Mr. Justice Secretary, we don't care whether the money you are "bribing" the Iloilo campaign leaders comes from your wife's chicken farm or from your neighbor's apog factory, it is still bribing. No more, no less. Well, folks, both our kababayans and OFWs who would be voting next week be prepared for possible election frauds. If history repeats, and it does, the Arroyo government will cheat again. It is almost a foregone conclusion from my own corner.

Let us all heed Jaro Archbishop Lagamaneo's exhortation: "We must disapprove, reject and condemn as immoral all acts of violence and cheating including the evil of vote padding and vote shaving, which is called dagdag-bawas in favor of or against any candidate." His appeal continues: "Let both candidates and their supports face the judgment of democratic election with humility and magnanimity." Let that appeal not be allowed to fall into the marsh of impertinence or irrelevance.

View 19

Let's Do Trillanes!

What an outsized surprise! He has been in a military detention now for four years, with no organization, no funds, no core political followers either in the military or in the national political front, Lt. SG Antonio Trillanes IV, has just realized his "impossible dream." Pretty soon, we hope, that he will be allowed by Pres. Arroyo to serve as a senator. His election despite all the political handicaps he faces, represents a celebration of spirit of Philippine democracy. It is a sad commentary that such exalted power of new vision for our country comes from the confines of a detention cell instead of from the halls of Malacanang. What a sorry picture indeed. Senator-elect rallying political campaign cry: CORRUPTON, CORRUPTION, CORRUPTON.

Former Sen. Honasan is fighting, according to the latest count, with Senator Ralph Recto as the tailender in the winning senatorial slate. So the final tally would be interesting to watch. There is already a spate of political speculation that Sen. Honasan might not make it after all and Sen. Recto wins, then the opposition is going hell crazy in accusing the Arroyo administration of cheating again. Incidentally, some observers have observed that perhaps Honasan should be blamed for his last-minute act of having to go to Malacanang and met Pres. Arroyo. Earlier, he has supposedly reviled and censured the opposition top leadership for not including him in the official GO senatorial

81

lineup. But whatever the outcome in the final analysis, Pres. Arroyo just got a heavy political thrashing.

Thanks to the last-minute strong endorsement of the GO candidates by detained President Estrada, former President Corazon Aquino, and the widow of Fernando Poe, Jr., Susan Roces.

The latest poll counts indicate that there could be 9-2-1 in the Senate, i.e., 9 GO, 2 independent and one TU, i.e., Sen. Joker Arroyo.

Detained Pres. Estrada appears to still command the support of the people. He endorses 11 GO candidates and they seemed certain of victory. Susan Roces' TV endorsement of Chiz Escudero and former Pres. Aquino helped catapult her son Noy Noy, in the winning column.

Senator Alfredo Lim has won all the 6 districts of Manila. He is now the next Mayor, a position he once served. Jejomar Binay also convincingly trounces his opponent. Some of Pres. Arroyo's rah rah boy and political fanatics who are trashed by the people in the poll: Former Pres. Ramos, Justice Secretary Raul Gonzalez, Executive Secretary Eduardo Ermita, presidential legal adviser Gabby Claudio and DILG Secretary Ronnie Puno. If delicadeza were to play in the their collective conscience, they all, except former Pres. Ramos, should tender their resignations for failing to deliver the "goods" to their most exalted leader Pres. Arroyo.

When the clouds of elections finally settled down, there should be an appropriate investigation on the disbursing of government funds to many of the administration candidates, both in the senate and local officials throughout the country. Reports indicate that Puno alone, receives from Malacanang the alleged amount of more than a billion pesos to help the administration political candidates.

Another big loser is Senator Ralph Recto. Poor Ralph, he put his foot in his mouth when he vociferously supported the highly controversial e-Vat issue.

Wonder whatever happens to the candidacy of the notorious wiretapped controversy player in "Hello, Garci" in which Pres. Arroyo was heard to have supposedly instructed him to cheat for her, Well, the former would-be Congress-man for the lst District of Bukidnon has just been hammered to defeat. He did not win despite the support of Malacanang. Manny "Pacman" Pacquiao was also severely upended by the Bukidnon voters despite the truck and truck-load of rice and other goodies throughout his district. One lesson to be learned is that celebrity status alone does not seem to hold political magic anymore. Illustrative lesson: Richard Gomez and Cesar Montano also lost. Tito Sotto whose presence in the TV land needs a giant HDT screen everyday also did not make it. All these celebrity losing candidates must now walk the cobbled political streets of repudiation.

Could this usher in a new era in Philippine politics. No more TV, screen actors and other celebrities in politics. Stay where you are good at, in the make-belief, celluloid world of acting where your filmic talent could be appreciated. Perhaps, the Filipino voters have become enlightened and astute in the exercise of their right to vote. Accept the money and run with it but vote according to your conscience!

As the vote tallying continues to come in, it appears that Pres. Arroyo has been taking a major political pounding. If the Senate remains in the hands of the opposition, then her abuses could be checked; if the TU candidates win, i.e., Mike Defensor, Migz Zubiri and Butch Pichay, she will stonewall any attempt to curb her abuse of power. No more IMPEACHMENT attempt hanging on her head.

Incidentally, Pres. Arroyo need not make a furious cry of political desperation. Her son, Dato Arroyo, won as congressman in the lst District of Camarines Sur by a comfortable margin. But in the case of Fr. Ed. Panlilio of Pampanga, Pres. Arroyo suffers a humiliating licking. This loss has been made more painful since Fr. Panlilio's campaign has been plagued with short cash flow.

If the pattern of voting continues to evolve, it appears that the congressional candidates of Pres. Arroyo's administration are going to win. So any attempt to resurrect the impeachment complaint will be unsuccessful again. But who knows the final counting might still see the victory of the congressional opposition candidates. If it does, and the Senate falls into the hands of the opposition, impeachment could very well be a reality yet.

Just whatever happens to the euphonious "unglories" of the "Hello, Garci" scandal? It is still haunting Pres. Arroyo, as well as General Ebdane, our National Secretary of National Defense, and General Esperon, our AFP chief of staff, two generals mentioned as having an unholy link with 2004 presidential cheating and trickery. They are also big losers here especially in the wash of Lt. Trillanes's victory. Honasan is still fighting with Sen. Recto at the cellar of the winning 12 magic circle.

View 20

Sen. Honasan vs. Justice Secretary Gonzalez
Legal Fisticuffs

Obviously, the Numero Uno lapdog of Pres. Arroyo is fuming mad as an aftermath of former Senator Honasan being released on cash bond of P200,000. On April 23, 2007, Justice Secretary Gonzalez lashes out at the Supreme Court for allegedly having "inspired a lower court into granting bail" to Sen Honasan who seems to have developed a gift of allegedly concocting coup attempt after coup attempt since the time of Pres. Corazon C. Aquino.

The ominous chill is lurking between the DOJ Secretary Gonzalez and SC Chief Justice Reynato Puno. No more balmy weather between the two top government officials of Pres. Arroyo. In a typical curt loud cry of an attack dog, Sec. Gonzalez barks out: "I am not happy with this (move on the rebellion case being faced by the former senator). He adds: "We're studying that (appealing the Makati RTC decision) and again we might be charged by some people that we are harassing him (Honasan). Being a realist, he adds: "I would think that a motion for reconsideration (on the bail grant) will not be successful."

Not merely trudging aimlessly on the matter of Honasan's bail, Sec. Gonzalez wonders aloud why the perceived would-be political slayer of Pres. Arroyo's government, Party-list Satur Ocampo is also granted bail by the lower court with the measly amount of P100,000. The

Justice secretary claims: "With the high tribunal allowing 'short cuts' (to be) granted (to) a favored person (Ocampo). I assume that the short cut must have convinced the courts such as the Makati RTC to also grant Honasan bail."

If you think Honasan's case is a simple one, well think some more. Secretary Gonzalez surmises that the other critics of Pres. Arroyo who have been charged in court would also be released as a result of the decision on the Honasan case.

Sec. Gonzalez deadpans some more on his sense of justice and fairness: "That is what I am afraid of. That Trillanes and Beltran will be allowed bail and all the efforts that we have done to safeguard the administration against destabilizers will have gone for naught." Listen Secretary Gonzalez, just belt to your heart's content the Phantom of the Opera song. Obviously he was referring to Lt/SG Antonio Trillanes IV and Party-List Rep. Crispin Beltran, both of whom are under detention at the moment.

Incidentally, Trillanes is also a senatorial candidate on the anti-Arroyo ticket (GO). So what will prevent former Pres. Joseph Estrada from posting bail, too! Well, Malacanang has a ready answer; "You see, Estrada is accused of plunder, and plunder, like rebellion, is non-bailable! There you are. Simple enough?

If my take is not exact edge-of-the-world legal analysis, why then Supreme Court Chief Justice is ordering the establishment of special courts to handle the cases involving extra-judicial killings of anti-administration individuals and a host of civil rights advocates.

More than a sliver of concern, the Supreme Court instructs the Court of Appeals to provide it with an inventory of extra-judicial killing cases. This latest attempt to determine the causes of the slaying of many human rights workers and leaders, opposition politicians and their followers, lawyers and journalists rippled from our highest court.

In an attempt to have a legal framework, Supreme Court Chief Justice Puno demands from the Court of Appeals Presiding Justice Ruben Reyes to conduct an inventory of such cases and then submit a report of its findings with the end in view to having "speed disposition."

The Supreme Court chief issues the order in response to the observation that numerous cases involving killings of political activists and members of the media have been filed and pending before the various courts in the country.

It is now clear that the Arroyo government is having difficulty navigating the choppy waters of national and international attention and denunciation.

In mid-April 2007, the International Union of Parliaments (IPU) is sending a three-member team to look into these slayings. The Inter-Parliamentary Union (IPU) is sending a fact-finding mission to the Philippines on April.18. Not too long ago, Bishop Beverly Shamana, head of a 16-member United Methodist Church of the United States California-Nevada Conference, which investigated the extra-judicial killings in the Philippines, issues a statement after their investigation: "We will urge US Senators and Congressmen to withdraw support for the Arroyo admin-istration of US government until the series of political assassinations in the country is resolved."

Philip Alston, United Nations (UN) Human Rights Commission, observes that the "Philippine military remains in state of almost total denial of its need to respond effectively and authentically to the significant number of killings attributed to it."

The International News Safety Institute (INSI) expresses grave concern over the assassination of members of the Philippine media.

Puno warns the judges of the trial courts throughout the country that failure to submit such inventory would be a ground for withholding the salaries and allowances of the judges, clerks of court and branch clerks of court concerned "without prejudice to whatever administrative sanction the SC may impose on them."

It comes to the attention of the Chief Justice Puno that an earlier set-up to try these heinous crimes is scuttled since even those judges involved are themselves being the targets of assassination!

In the current SC plan, there would be three special courts each in Manila, Quezon City, and Makati City and two each in the cities of Pasay, Caloocan and Pasig.

Under the SC guidelines, the special courts may determine whether the crime is a "political killing" by considering the political affiliation of the victim, method of attack, as well as reports that state agents were involved in the commission of the crime." The SC orders continuous trial of such cases, which shall be terminated within 60 days from commencement of the hearing.

Why this sudden interest of the Philippine Supreme Court in the extra-judicial slayings in the country? It appears that the Arroyo administration is under international pressures to take some tangible and visible steps to project an image to the critics, especially to the leaders of international human rights organizations that Pres. Arroyo is sincere in her promise to solve these killings.

Several international organizations are gearing up in investigating these assassinations. UN Human Rights Commission Rapporteur Philip Alston who went to the Philippines to conduct an investigation on the matter, is scheduled to submit his findings to the United Nations Human Rights Council (UNHRC). He is expected to reveal his findings in a speech he would be making before the 4th session of the UNHRC to be held in Geneva, Switzerland.

Senator Sharon Costairs of Canada and IPU Secretary General Anders Johnsson may join the fact-finding team. It was also recently reported that the European Commission (EC), executive body of the European Union (EU) is contemplating to send its own investigating team to the Philippines soon. The US State Department is also sending a fact-finding team.

Due to this development, the slow-creeping wheels of justice insofar as the extra-judicial assassinations are concerned would have to move faster this time. The Arroyo can no longer afford to move in halting or faltering manner since the world community has finally taken cognizance of the disturbing human rights violations in the Philippines.

View 21

Peninsula Hotel Abortive Siege

The fast breaking news as gathered from CNN coverage yesterday, November 29, indicated that another military "rebellion" took place at Makati. The rebel soldiers used another 5-star hotel Peninsula as their headquarters and "beachhead." They were demanding the resignation of Pres. Arroyo. Latest news indicates that it is a short-lived military "rebellion." After all the hotel guests were safely evacuated the military rebels immediately surrendered after a military tank rammed through the main entrance of the hotel lodging tear gas canisters. Preliminary reports indicated that several opposition leaders and newspapermen were arrested. Manila is literally locked down, i.e., no public transportation and curfew was imposed. Schools – both public and private – were closed.

Regardless of the outcome of this latest military flare-up, it is definitely symptomatic of the "malignancy" literally eating the will and discipline of our military. It appears that demanding Pres. Arroyo to resign is fast becoming a mouthwatering motivation for some "disgruntled" military officers and men to engage in abortive after abortive military adventurism. There is another factor that feeds the jitters in military camps and he is the current AFP Chief of Staff Gen. Esperon, Jr. Esperon is becoming an inspiration for a wave of simmering protests for change in the military leadership because of his "unquestionable" loyalty to Pres.

Arroyo. As a result both Pres. Arroyo and Gen. Esperon are becoming the symbol of what is ailing our Republic. As long as Pres. Arroyo remains president, Esperon will become the lightning rod for military discontent, which could result in the final destabilization of the Arroyo government. Both inspired a wave for clamor to have "regime change" in our Republic.

This latest Hotel Peninsula failed military "coup" could very well be considered a warning shot (and more warning shots to be heard in the future?) across the bow of a beleaguered Arroyo administration.

As a backgrounder, the following information is shared with our readers:

On October 10, 2007, the Young Enlisted Soldiers Active and Retired Military-Police for Solidarity (YES ARM) releases a statement through its spokesman retired Commodore Ismael Aparri declaring that the public perception of AFP Chief of Staff Esperon Jr. is so negative that his only recourse is to resign. The main reason: Gen. Esperon is one of the four generals who are allegedly involved in rigging the presidential election returns in 2004. This information is gathered through the "Hello, Garci" wiretap.

A supposed investigation is conducted by a military panel headed by AFP Inspector General Mateo Mayuga regarding the alleged involvement of Gen. Esperon and other generals in the 2004 cheating. After the investigation, a report known as the Mayuga Report is allegedly submitted to AFP and Malacanang. However, the contents of the report are not made public. The government justification: The Mayuga Report could jeopardize the national security of the country! To Pres. Arroyo's critics, the national security excuse is a convenient reason that encircles the remaining bastion of cover-up by the Arroyo government.

Aparri counters that it has no basis at all. He claims that many members of the AFP and the PNP, both officers and troopers, demand that Esperon reveal the content of the Mayuga Report for "ethical reasons and fair play."

The YES ARM spokesman declares that "this is not about national security that when the Mayuga Report is revealed to the public it will cause undue harm to the nation. The truth must be out, heads should roll and justice must not be denied our people. The scheming government has brought an injustice to our idealist men in uniform and to our hapless poor." The Mayuga Report findings are not surprising at all. Esperon and all the generals mentioned in the "Hello, Garci" controversial wiretap have been exonerated!

On November 10, the reforming group YES ARM again demands Esperon to step down declaring that his prolonged "stay in office is fueling disgust and open disobedience from the idealist men in uniform, a development which could escalate and end up destabilizing the Arroyo government." In a phone interview the following day, Aparri claims Esperon is violating the law, citing the first in the history of the military service where the former refuses to sign the pre-trial advice (PTA) which could legally allow the court-martial proceedings against military officers who allegedly took part in a supposedly attempt for withdrawal of support from Pres. Arroyo in February 2006 to be carried out.

Aparri contends that this Esperon refusal is expected since the pre-trial investigators recommend that the alleged military plotters be dealt with less harsher action under the Articles of War. Of course, Esperon does not like it. Aparri continues: "Esperon junked it and proceeded to create the general court martial because he wants harsher penalties equivalent to death designed to torture our idealists men in uniform, now he refuses to sign the PTA on the flimsy excuse that he does not need to sign it, since he has already signed up a memorandum authorizing the creation of a general court-martial. But that's absurd and against the law. It's an easy way out for him to escape prosecution in the future." Aparri notes that without the signature of Esperon on the PTA, any general court martial proceeding would be a "sham and would leave the detained soldiers and their rights as accused gravely abused." He elaborates further: "Unless he (Esperon) quits his post now, sympathizers of the idealists soldiers detained would grow in number until the bubble of insurgency bursts. He's in open violation of the rules of court and how he mishandled the AFP is contributing to the demoralization of the men in uniform. It encourages rebellious attitude toward the AFP leadership."

The civilian lawyers of the accused officers of military plot to overthrow the Arroyo government demand that Esperon sign the PTA. However, Esperon stubbornly refuses to do so. The accused military officers are led by former Marines commandant Maj. Gen. Renato Miranda, former First Scout Ranger Regiment commander Brig. Gen. Danilo Lim and Medal of Valor awardees Marines Col. Ariel Querubin and Marines Lt. Col. Custodio Parcon, along with all the other officers, walked out of the courtroom last week to protest the court's alleged bias. One of the civilian lawyers who walks out with the accused military officers is former solicitor general Cesar Chavez who serves under Pres. Corazon Aquino.

View 22

Impeachment And The Stealing Of The Presidency

Impeach Pres. Gloria Macapagal-Arroyo? No way. No how. Even if she steals Mt. Arayat and Mt. Pinatubo, too, she will get away with it. Even under the pale shadow of brainless and stupid political circumstances in our home country, Pres. Arroyo will stay in power until 2010, unless she decides to change the Constitution by dancing the CHA CHA waltz. Between now and May 2010, she might still pull this disgusting strategy. But then the military might very well provoke the collective wrath of the people to topple down Pres. Arroyo's corrupt government.

As long as Mr. Noli de Castro remains her vice president, her political luck will not leave her. Unlike in 2001, when then Pres. Joseph "Erap" was at the brink of being impeached, his vice president was Gloria Macapagal-Arroyo, an American-educated PEPE (Political Elite of Philippine Elections), with a doctorate degree in economics, to boot. Since Pres. Estrada, according to his political detractors, is a college dropout, politically "uncouth" and lacking social graces and needed sobriety, along with being unrepentant womanizer, impeaching or better still "overthrowing" him by the effete elite of Philippine society in cahoots with the movers and shakers of business and industry, is not too difficult to contemplate. In fact it has been done. Forcibly throwing out of power is made easy and "legally" palatable with the cooperation and sanction of the Supreme Court presided by Chief Justice Hilario Davide. Many critics of the Arroyo government feel that the Davide Court hastens the "overthrow" of then Pres. Estrada. It is not difficult to strip Pres. Estrada of power since Vice-President Macapagal is lurching around. An educated lady.

After three impeachment attempts in the House of Representatives, one may ask why she is still president considering the litany of corruption charges against her administration. The latest unsuccessful third impeachment salvo made her insulated for another year. Such is the luck of our "Teflon President."

Why? One reason is because of Vice-President Noli D. Castro. As long as he is the second in command, the Lady Chief Executive will stay in Malacanang. Imagine the would-be president has a pending bigamy case filed by no less than the children of his current "wife." Imagine the pretender to the presidency has questionable academic records, i.e., many allege that his supposed college degree is bogus. That he has no record in public service except being a "bayan ko" radio broadcaster deft in reading flawlessly the teleprompter. His political success, to many observers, from being catapulted to the senate and chosen by presidential candidate Mrs. Arroyo is like pulling off a breathtaking political miracle. Or is it? Many critics, particularly the elite members of the Philippine society along with business leaders consider Vice-Pres. De Castro a bad political replacement tire. He is bereft of leadership potential with utter lack of charisma. So why change Pres. Arroyo with Vice-Pres. De Castro.

Quezon City Rep. Matias Defensor Jr., chairman of the House committee on justice declares recently that while he "believes that the members of the minority did not sleep on their job in trying to remove Mrs. Arroyo, the President herself did not commit any impeachable offense." Whoa!

And then with uncontrollable glee, he continues" "You can very clearly see that based on the reaction of the people regarding the impeachment complaint, there was no mass hysteria as compared to the impeachment complaint against former President Joseph Estrada where people from all walks of life came out." With De Castro waiting in the wings to be our next president, just exactly why would the Filipinos from "all walks of life" would come out and cheer! As a matter of fact, three weeks ago, the same elite Filipinos and political cognoscenti shamelessly suggest that the Philippine should be ruled by a sort of a "junta" headed by Chief Justice of the Supreme Court Puno, who by the way is a member of the Davide Court which hurriedly anointes with indecent dispatch Pres. Arroyo in 2001.

One must recall that in 2001, there is no plenary vote in the House of Representatives. The impeachment complaint against Pres. Estrada is done posthaste and in lickety-split manner sent to the Senate for "trial." Talking of bad hair day for then Pres. Estrada!

On November 26, or before the third impeachment report is presented to the plenary, Paranaque Rep. Roilo Golez, a former cabinet member of Pres. Arroyo and now a senior minority leader in the House of Representatives voices the opposition stand to boycott or snub by declaring: "The minority will continue its boycott of the impeachment complaint when the matter is reported out today for plenary debate." He then elaborates: "It is not the duty of the minority to fight for what we have believed right the very start as a sham impeachment complaint. We will just watch the charade and see how Rep. San Luis will fight for his impeachment complaint. The opposition in the House is not a mindless opposition that would be drawn into a battle that is not its own making."

One unexpected political drama took place. One congressman who abstained in the viva voce voting. Nueva

Ecija Representative Edno Joson justifies his abstention. "I don't believe there is a thing such as a sham complaint...An impeachment complaint, whether it is weak or whatever, always boils down to numbers." Amen.

In countering the opposition boycott, Rep. Edgar San Luis, is deeply disappointed when the opposition decides to snub the plenary voting. He laments: "It's rather unfortunate that the opposition decided to boycott the impeachment almost all the way... But even then, I have already been expecting that since Day One. The position on the impeachment was very clear even though I have been very cooperative ...and was even willing to withdraw my endorsement of the Roel Pulido impeachment complaint provided they (opposition) substituted it with their own. Had the opposition not walked out of the hearing, we could have raised the issue of the form and forced it to be returned back to the complainant therefore paving the way for the Adel Tamano (supplemental) complaint to be incorporated." What a Jacobean political rhetoric!

In the meanwhile, the matter of the Tamano supplemental impeachment complaint is now in the Supreme Court. Will the Supreme Court give the ultimate, final primal stink to the entire sordid political drama?

View 23

Who Is Coming Back Like An Old Song?

Former Elections Commissioner Virgilio Garcillano, that's who.

The prospect of being the subject of the Senate Committee on Whole investigation of the "Hello, Garci" wiretap controversy must be causing Pres. Arroyo to twist in the winds right now. Current developments in the Senate appear to be developing the clawing reach of potential political bombshell.

One must remember that the "Hello, Garci" firestorm did not only involve a simple case of wiretapping of conversations Pres. Arroyo had with a political constituent. She is allegedly caught in a compromising phone chat urging Elections Commissioner Garcillano to cheat in Lanao with a margin of "more than 1 million votes' plurality" to insure her "victory" over opposition candidate Fernando Poe, Jr. That's a criminal act committed by no less than the president.

Pres. Arroyo is so concerned, better still is so afraid that this "Hello, Garci" flap could cause her downfall, a shameful descent from power – even being sent into a lock up. No, it must never happen, she must have said to herself. So she attempts to change our Constitution into a parliamentary system so that she could avoid being investigated in the Senate. Remember the failed CHA CHA? Another is her successful attempts (twice in fact) to stymie her impeachment. It is accomplished with the political influence and political aplomb of House Speaker De Venecia. In the seven boxes of evidence which would have been presented during the impeachment proceedings in the House, is the proof that she cheats in the May 2004 presidential elections. It too, fails to unseat her.

But in the wake of the victory of the GO opposition senatorial candidates, the "Hello, Garci" dispute, some sort of the political argy-bargy of Pres. Arroyo's supposed chicanery and duplicity, the Senate would soon start issuing summons to individuals, present and former government officials, even high-ranking military officers, to appear and testify before the Senate Committee on the Whole.

Starting next week, the "Hello, Garci" Senate investigation would commence. The results could come to a boil in the end. The star witness, former Intelligence Service agent T/Sgt. Vidal Doble, Jr. would be joined by a new witness. This is revealed by Senator Rodolfo Biazon last week in the Kapihan sa Senado.

Sen. Biazon says: "This witness has actually voluntarily submitted to us during the hearings ... three tapes, one supposed to be the original Garci tap, the wiretapped tape of the office of Sen. Honasan and the wiretapped of the office of Sen. Lacson, because at the time he (Lacson) was running for president and these (tapes) were submitted to us, accompanied by an affidavit of the witness describing the circumstances of each receipt of these three tapes."

The forthcoming Senate probe would be handled by Senators Biazon, Cayetano, the chairman of the Senate of the Blue Ribbon Committee and Richard Gordon, chair of the Electoral Reforms Committee.

The Senate investigating committee could summon at least three of the so-called "four Garci generals" allegedly involved in the supposed tampering of election returns in Lanao. These generals include former AFP Chief of Staff

Efren Abu, former Isafp chief Tirso Danga and Roy Kyamko. If Garcillano, and the retired generals refuse to testify, the Senate could order their arrest. Reason: they are all out of the government service, hence the Malacanang executive order prohibiting government officials from attending any senate probe without the approval of Pres. Arroyo herself.

The lawyer of retired Sgt Doble, Alex Avisado provides an intriguing, if riveting comment last week: "Given the chance, I think he (Doble) will drop more bombs."

In my book: CALL FOR TRUE DEMOCRACY (order through AMAZON.COM and BARNESNOBLE.COM), I have the following excerpts: 'HELLO, GARCI,' A CATCH-AS-CATCH CAN CALL. Frankly, I am choked with disgust, Madam President, to contemplate the fate and whereabouts of former Commissioner of Elections Virgilio Garcillano. ... the fundamental question I am asking – and will continue to ask – is, "Where is Commissioner Garcillano?" You and your advisers should not be allowed to continue blustering and bluffing your merry way without determining the whereabouts of your former commissioner of elections. This is a ghost that will continue to haunt you. Commissioner Garcillano is a principal witness who can throw light on your alleged cheating in the May 2004 elections....As long as the commissioner is "missing," the Filipino people will believe that you are robbing us silly. The sycophants of Malacanang cannot continue to stonewall on this question. Will this Garcillano controversial ultimately bring your administration to a sticky end?"

Incidentally, I also include in my book my picture at the foot of the Aquino Monument in Makati, with a big banner announcing: 'HELLO, GARCI" CHEATING IS THE PROBLEM NOT CHA CHA, STUPID!"

View 24

Love Of Country – More Edifying

Something interesting about this abortive "coup" at Peninsula Hotel. It starts when Trillanes, Lim and former Vice-President Guingona along with members of the Magdalo officers and soldiers who participated in the Oakwood "mutiny" in 2003 walk out from the court hearing in the Makati Regional Trial Court. Trillanes group walk nearly 3 kilometers; it takes them more than 2 hours to negotiate the distance between the court and the Peninsula Hotel. The military security marches with them without stopping the marchers. Upon arrival in Peninsula Hotel, the military soldiers who are supposedly with Trillanes group force their way inside the luxury hotel without much difficulty. While three bishops joined the march and stayed inside the hotel, one wonders why at least 2 vocal Catholic prelates who are bitter critics of the president, i.e., Bishops Antonio Tobias and Deogracias Yniguez, were not in the Hotel.

The mass arrest of the media people present in the Hotel cause some concern. Why would these newsmen who are in the hotel to cover the evolving story are rounded up and held for 36 hours. Another rather disturbing development is the imposition of curfew and the announcement by the military that the Peninsula Hotel failed coup is part of a larger conspiracy to "topple the Arroyo government." Oh, what servile self-seeking flatterers among the police and military would do to inveigle themselves to the president!

As regards Makati Mayor Jojo Binay, it is good that he did not proceed to the hotel to find out the demands of the "plotters." Had he gone to the hotel he could have been slapped with rebellion charge with no bail granted. Guingona is one of those being held without bail. If the Arroyo paranoia is allowed to grow unchecked, many more anti-government critics could later be apprehended and detained without bail. If this political psychosis is not stopped, prominent political opposition leaders could be hauled to jail later.

As the aftermath of Peninsula Hotel episode, Malacanang will weave a bigger thread of conspiracy. Military intelligence would come up with "participants," who could be arrested later. This sends chilling warning to political detractors of Pres. Arroyo. They still could find themselves being charged with rebellion and held without bail.

One member of the Magdalo mutineers Captain Nicanor Faeldon is now being hunted down with financial reward to individuals who could provide information that could lead to his capture. There is one million-peso bounty on his head. The military intelligence alleges that Capt Faeldon is inside the Manila Peninsula but is able to flee before the surrender of Sen. Trillanes.

This propensity of the Arroyo government to offer a reward for information leading to the arrest of suspected rebels is well known. But in many cases, these financial rewards are given to military or retired military men pretending to be bounty hunters. Since they have all the needed intelligence, they could "capture" and "surrender" suspected rebels and receive the rewards, which could be divided or shared by some spurious "hunters" who are mostly military or retired police personnel.

View 25

The Whereabouts Of The Peninsula 36

Where are the Peninsula Hotel 36 "coup plotters" now?

Immediately after their arrest, the Armed Forces of the Philippine orders them transferred from the detention facility in Camp Bagong Diwa in Taguig City to a maximum security holding center in Camp Crame, Quezon City.

As if worried that the "thunder of feet" to escape and "tumult" of persistent desire to bolt out of detention, Malacanang instructs the military authorities to move these coup conspirators to New Bilibid Prison in Muntinlupa. If this move pushes through, all the Peninsula 36 would be behind bars in a crowded, rotten prison with hardened criminals.

Marius Corpus, DILG Undersecretary for Public Safety announces that the government prosecutors will ask the courts to transfer Sen. Trillanes and Army Brig. Gen. Danilo Lim and others who were all charged with non-bailable crime of rebellion, to be remanded to the Muntinlupa facilities. Corpus gives the following reason: 'We have studied the matter carefully and weighed the factors regarding the safety and security of the accused, and decided that the best way to secure them while they are awaiting the trial of their rebellion case is to house them in Muntinlupa."

"Security" and "safety" you say? Tell that to the Marines, say many Arroyo critics. To them it is pure and unadulterated vindictiveness. What is interesting about human behavior is that those incarcerated always have on their minds the "shadow" of escape laying "upon their sleep." Could this be applied to the Peninsula 36?

Another justification being peddled by the military authorities: "Because rebellion is not a violation of the Articles of War but of the Revised Penal Code, we have to house them in a civilian facility, so this also rules out the possible transfer of custody of Trillanes and his co-accused soldiers to the military."

Those being considered for Muntinlupa "Peninsula" Prison include Lt. Junior Grade Arturo Pascua Jr., Capt. Gary Lejano, Capt. Segundino Orfiano Jr., Lt. Senior Grade James Layug, Lt. Eugene Peralta, Lt. SG Manuel Cabochan, Lt. Andy Torrato PFC German Linde Manuel, Ensign Armando Pontejos and 1st Lt Billy Bascua. 1st Lt Jonnel Sanggalang, First Class Emmanuel Tirador, PFC Juanito Jilbury, and Corporal Clecarte Dahan,

Four high profile civilian personalities had been released: former Vice President Teofisto Guingona Jr., Bishop Julio Labayen, former University of the Philippines president Francisco Nemenzo and Elizabeth Orteza Siguion Reyna. While these individuals are released by PNP, they nevertheless will be charged with rebellion. But I thought rebellion is a non-bailable crime?

Guingona is placed under the custody of his wife; Labayen is released to the Catholic Bishops Conference of the Philippines (CBCP), Nemenzo to the custody of UP authorities and Orteza to her mother-in-law, Armida Seguion Reyna, sister of Senator Juan Ponce Enrile.

Other civilians charged with rebellion: lawyers JV Bautista and Argee Guevarra, Myna Buendia and Leodor de la Cruz, Dominador Ireneo Rull Jr., Julius Mesa, Romeo Solis, Roel Gaduin, Rhonnmel Rivero, Julian Advincula, Francisco Bosi, Sonny Madarang, Cesar Yassir, Francisco Penaflor and Antonio Trillanes III, brother of Sen. Trillanes.

View 26

The Anti-Subversion Law: A Cruel Ploy

Eerily the Marcos repressive era suddenly streaks the Philippine sky of an equally abusive and corrupt government of Pres. Arroyo. She is behaving like she is looking for an excuse to stay in power beyond 2010. It is like a shadow of the past laying upon the present. Is Martial Law asserting its crisp sound bite?

Sorsogon Rep. Jose Solis is introducing a bill in the House of Representatives, which seeks to resurrect the Anti-Subversive Law of former dictator Pres. Ferdinand E. Marcos. The deposed dictator uses it effectively to quell opposition to his rule that lasted for 20 years. During the Marcos regime, the law is utilized supposedly to check the spread of communism but in its wake it becomes a brutal instrument to crush public dissent.

It also allows the military (remember Gen. Fabian Ver?) to have the arbitrary power to run after the communist elements that in the end it becomes a carte blanche of blatant human rights abuses by the military. Top military operatives of Pres. Marcos act as if they have license to kill.

The leaders of the Pambansang Lakas ng Kilusang Mamamalakaya ng Pilipinas (Pamalakaya) quickly denounce Rep. Solis for his legislative initiative. Critics of the President claim that Malacanang is behind the move. But Pres. Arroyo is giving the impression that she is "distancing" from Rep. Solis plan. Nonetheless, the lady commander-in-chief expresses "support" for the move to revive the Anti-Subversion Law. Press Secretary and presidential spokesman Bunye declares that if "this initiative of Representative Solis is endorsed by the Local Peace and Security Assembly (LPSA), she (Pres. Arroyo) would have no objection (to it)." What a richly detailed portrait of political doublespeak only Pres. Arroyo could ever concoct.

House minority deputy leader Paranaque Rep. Golez, a graduate of the U.S. Naval Academy, gives a stern warning to Pres. Arroyo arguing that reviving a "dead law" which has been scrapped by Pres. Fidel Ramos could "backlash at the country's democratic system." Rep. Golez, reminds "that history repeat itself. That's true. But the march of history is irreversible. That's more true and the repeal of the anti-subversion law is irreversible. We cannot ban ideology. We compete with it in the free market of ideas and prove that espousing capitalism and democracy is better for the country than being a member of the Communist Party of the Philippines which the Anti-Subversion banned before 1992." Golez adds that when Gen. Fidel Ramos, a graduate of the U.S. Military Academy, is the chief of the Philippine Constabulary, during the Marcos regime, he enforces the Anti-Subversion Law, i.e., fighting the communist NPAs.

But when he becomes president, he repeals the Anti-Subversion Law. Ironically, Pres. Ramos' trusted ally then, Rep. Eduardo Ermita, a Philippine Military Academy graduate, authors the bill repealing the Anti-Subversion Law. Now Ermita is now one of the closest advisers of Pres. Arroyo. After its repealed, the New People's Army's strength is reduced.

One of the top advisers of Pres. Marcos is former Senator Francisco Tatad. He now feels that the restoration of the Anti-Subversion Law is "not the solution to the insurgency problem." Sen. Loren Legarda, being groomed to be a would-be presidential wannabe in 2010, shares her concern about the "big number of political killings and disappearances in the country." She expresses the fear that such restoration of the Anti-Subversion Law could lead to "martial law." Sen. Legarda argues that such "monstrous Anti-Subversion Law could only make the situation worse and drive more people underground. Her solution: "reduce or alleviate grinding poverty" of the large segments of the Filipino people. Well taken. Bravo!

We cannot chop away successfully communist insurgency when poverty is eating up the very belly of the Filipino people. Extreme economic deprivation is taking a painful toll in our country. Reports of young children from impoverished families committing suicides are not uncommon. Anti-Subversion Law cannot be a remedy to such socio-economic malaise of our kababayans. It is not a hedge against poverty.

View 27

Military Role In The Elections Berated By International Monitors

On June 12, 2007, the 12-nation international election observer group assails the very visible and rather unsettling "presence" of the military during the May 14 elections. This spectacle is played out in many places throughout the country. The international monitors claim that such obtrusive bordering open meddling is a reminiscent of the 2004 presidential elections. Just as in 2004, the international monitoring group is quick to call for independent investigation on the conduct of the 2004 national elections with the view to resolving the question surrounding the legitimacy of the Pres. Arroyo's presidency.

In the face of the accusation leveled by the People's International Observer's Mission (IOM), it behooves the government to look into the matter. The international group of monitors observes pointedly: "Extra-judicial killings of political partisans campaigning for and against particular candidates, disenfranching voters of opposition candidates, intimidation and harassment, deployment in opposition-influenced communities are many of the ways that the military used and overstepped its constitutional duty." Seeing military soldiers in full battle gears guarding sentries did not exactly attenuate the apprehension of the people trying to cast their votes.

One may consider that such accusation is a collage of a fragment of the political sin of the Arroyo administration of the past. But the IOM observers believe that it is becoming a pattern of fraud and rigging of national elections in the Philippines.

IOM cites the following bullying and intimidating tactics of the military in the last May 14 elections 1) military checkpoints are encountered by the IOM team and one team has been stopped twice, questioned, their names listed down and their photographs taken by the soldiers against their will, 2) general chaos, irregularities and vulnerabilities to manipulation of poll results.

Meanwhile, Lintang Bedol, PBC chairman, and Comelec Commissioner for Mindanao claims that the MCoC are "stolen from his office last May 29." Bedol adds: "Before they could be transmitted to Manila, they got lost. How they got lost, I do not know." Easy for you to say! Interestingly enough, while he claims that they are stolen, he reports that there has been "no break-in."

When queried why he fails to answer the subpoena to appear before the National Board of Canvassers (NBC) last May 30, he explains that the subpoena is sent to his election officers, not to him. Lawyer Bedol unfazed by a barrage of questions from the media continues to elaborate: "These are the things that I cannot understand because the only hearing where I was given a directive is that one in May 25. On May 30, I did not appear because I was not given a subpoena. It was my election officer in the 22 municipalities who was given the subpoena instead. So it would be wrong for a field officer to come to Manila without a copy of a directive without a subpoena because you will not be able to reimburse your expenses." Woe isn't to Bedol, if he is in fact telling the truth!

Commissioner Bedol is not flinching at the possible non-ethical energies of the Comelec reported inability to prevent cheating and chaos in his area of jurisdiction. Bedol claims further unabashedly: "The election in Maguindanao were peaceful." As if it is a statement worthy of carving it on a stone from Siquijor, he crows brazenly: "That my statement should be proof that there was no electoral fraud in Maguindanao." If you believe that, then believe also that there are aswang (witches) in Capiz (now Roxas). That would be pushing believability to the edge of impertinence.

Follow his political syllogistic mental gymnastics: "Our statement is already proof that there was no cheating in Maguindanao, unless that statement is controverted by another statement supported by evidence, strong enough to convince us that there was cheating then that's the only time we will believe there was fraud."

If you are not sufficiently shocked or offended then listen some more to Bedol's fulmination: "Candidates getting zero votes is not impossible in Mindanao." He then continues his insolent musing: "There is such a thing as command votes, which gives rivals zero." Enough already!

View 28

"Impeach Me Again!"

Are we Filipinos real-life fools or simply borderline nutcase of a people to believe that Pres. Arroyo did not know the giving of the bundles of cash in Malacanang on October 31? "Not me," barks Sen. Richard Gordon, who is supposed to be an ardent ally of our "extremely generous" Lady Chief Executive in the Senate. The brown-bagging of thousands of millions taking place within the confines of the Palace!

On November 10, the Senator from Subic, a member of good standing of the Kabalikat ng Malayang Pilipino (KAMPI), which is headed by Pres. Arroyo, shamelessly observes: "It is hard to believe that money, from P200,000 to P500,000, was being distributed without anyone telling anyone what it was for and where it had come from...even harder to believe that the President, who we assume is also the leader of Kampi, did not know that money was being distributed like rain or sunshine." What a postcard-perfect backdrop of naked bribery of our Congressmen and local officials! It is corroding our faith in our president.

Ah, are we seeing the political tumbledown ruin of Pres. Arroyo? But let us all be reminded that the "cash only" distribution is made in Malacanang on the day Atty Pulido filed an "impeachment" complaint. Why the sudden "generosity" to 190 congressmen and more than 50 local executives? The Pulido-initiated "impeachment" complaint is supposed to be a political ploy to inoculate or insulate

Pres. Arroyo from the real impeachment for another year or until she steps down (if she does) in 2010.

Nabuking na naman si Ate Gloria! (Pres. Arroyo stumbles again). On November 11, a 60-page supplemental impeach complaint is filed by the United Opposition (UNO) lawyer Adel Tamano before the House of Representatives. In 2005 and 2006, the opposition ignominiously suffers twice-told defeats. This time, a second supplemental impeachment rap has been filed by the militant party-list Bayan Muna, Anakpawis and Gabriela which is supposed to be more comprehensive and all-embracing in reach and scope. The second supplemental rap is anchored on the belief that Pres. Arroyo is the mastermind of the sham impeachment designed to immunize her from a real impeachment complaint. The rationale of the second impeachment complaint: "The proceeding is to expose the criminality, the illegality and the unconstitutionality of the conduct in the Office of the Chief Executive – the highest official in the land – and is aimed to uphold the Constitution, the Rule of Law and the accountability of the President to the Filipino people, the true Sovereign of the Republic of the Philippines."

During this time of spiraling scandals allegedly involving Pres. Arroyo and her husband (in the ZTE National Broadband scandal), it is very difficult to have moonlit strolls in the Palace by the Pasig River. Pres. Arroyo's bogus almsgiving to protect her political hide is starting to smell fetid and as noxious and smelly as Pasig River during the summer time.

Another interesting, but disgusting development that takes place when the opposition supplemental impeach rap is filed before the Committee of Justice in the House of Representatives whose majority members are Pres. Arroyo's political allies. UNO attorney Tamano states that a "staff of the committee received his complaint and had it stamped only to later ask him to return his receiving copy saying they were not allowed to accept the supplemental complaint." Whether the House Committee on Justice will accept or not the supplemental complaint, Tamano argues: "The rule under the House Rule in submitting supplementary amendment to an impeachment rap is clear." The "amendment extinguishes an original complaint. A supplement substantiates an existing complaint, or if there are new events or facts that occur after the filing of the complaint, then you are allowed to supplement." However, the administration members of the House of Representative Justice Committee reiterate that such filing of supplemental complaint would "only be rendered useless as the impeachment against the President had already been initiated with its endorsement by De Venecia to the Justice Committee, and as such, no other complaints can be entertained until the one year ban expires." What an otherwordly clever political rationalization! And yet Malacanang has doggedly denied that Pres. Arroyo is behind the move to throw out the opposition supplemental impeachment complaint. Says Ronaldo Puno, the Interior and Local Government Secretary: "To tell you the truth, President Arroyo was not involved" in the cash gift distribution. No outburst of misplaced presidential generosity here? What a tete-a-tete of unbelievability!

In the meanwhile, while no less than the Minority Leader Rep. Ronnie Zamora has pointed out that there could be a legal issue or technicality in filing the supplemental impeachment rap, he was quick in pointing out that at the end of the day, the Supreme Court could decide the acceptability or legality of the supplemental complaint.

Ang anak nga naman! (son is always a son of a father). Just because Pres. Arroyo pardoned his father, Erap Estrada, Sen. Jinggoy Estrada had the temerity to comment on November 5: "Why not let President Arroyo finish her term until 2010." To which opposition Rep. Rufus Rodriguez, one time close ally of former Pres. Estrada retorts: "He (Sen. Jinggoy Estrada) should be wary of what he says because he might assume the role of a jury member if ever the impeachment complaint against GMA is elevated to the Senate. He should not make statement which could prejudge or precondition the impeachment proceedings if ever this pushes through."

Amid the political imbroglio being created by the filing of supplemental impeachment rap, waiting in the wings is the role of the military in insuring that the will of the Filipino people should be respected or uphold. It has been said that "as fire kindled by bellows, so is anger by words." But in the case of the military frame of mind or military regimentation, anger could be kindled by arms! Just thinking aloud.

View 29

Look, Who's Talking?

During her attendance at the UN 62nd General Assembly, Pres. Arroyo urges Myanmar repressive regime to "redeem democracy" in the military junta-ruled Southeast Asian nation formerly known as Burma.

Pres. Arroyo intones: "Recent events in Myanmar, therefore, are of concern to the Philippines and to the region as a whole. The Philippines asks the government of Myanmar to act with utmost restraint and to take immediate steps to preserve the advances that have been made in its roadmap to democracy."

"We call on Myanmar to act on its own best interest to avoid its further isolation and to redeem its democracy without any further delay. We have patiently but persistently advised Myanmar within ASEAN (Association of South East Asian Nations) that it must make greater and faster progress toward that goal. Specifically, we ask the government of Myanmar to now allow all interested parties to take full part in the effort to national reconciliation through peaceful and inclusive dialog. This means the release of all those who have been detained and who can contribute to the process of national renewal, including Ms. Aung San Suu Kyi," Pres. Arroyo piously exhorts.

Let's give the benefit of the doubt to Pres. Arroyo. Perhaps she means well. But it is very difficult to believe her when in our country, human rights advocates, opposition leaders, lawyers and journalists are being systematically harassed, abducted and even murdered with appalling impunity. There is more than a strain of hypocrisy in her statement.

To her detractors, her exhortation is tad bogus lacking even the most rudiment aspect of sincerity. In fact her advice smacks more than a sniff of ironic mockery. Look at the imprisonment or disappearance of those who oppose her government policies since she assumes power in 2001.

Is it possible that our country could be ruled by a military junta soon? Disturbing developments are shaping up in the Philippines. Gen. Esperon appears to be building his military power base. His appointment of retired Vice-Admiral Tirso Danga, the former Intelligence czar at the time of the wiretapping of the phone calls between Pres. Arroyo and Election Commissioner Garcillano who like him was tagged as one of the "Hello, Garci" generals could signal some ominous developments. If the rest of the "Hello, Garci" generals (most are now retired) were appointed to positions in Malacanang Palace, it certainly deserves concern. It is ominous.

Two possible scenarios that could evolve. 1) Pres. Arroyo herself would declare martial law when the political noose is starting to tighten around her neck. Of course, it would be done with the assistance of AFP Chief Gen. Esperon. 2) Gen. Esperon himself with the active participation and connivance of his generals (especially those identified with the "Hello, Garci" scandal), could unilaterally grab power from the President. After all, what can the lady president do when her top military generals decide to consign her to the dustbin of political oblivion. Exile perhaps! Or worse.

For the first time in many years, the Speaker of the House did not accompany the president to the United Nations Assembly. Why is House Speaker Jose De Venecia not included in the official entourage of Pres. Arroyo? Could it be because the Speaker's son, Jose III is involved in the ZTE broadband anomaly? A source of embarrassment for the president?

Some political gurus predict that Pres. Arroyo would be impeached successfully this time around. Third impeachment attempt could be a charm. If the reported parting of ways between Pres. Arroyo and House Speaker De Venecia is true, then the latter needs only "solid 40" congressmen all loyal to him to impeach the lady chief executive. The congressional opposition blocks would be more than excited to vote for Pres. Arroyo's impeachment. Waiting in the Upper Chamber are the ecstatic Senators (there are more opposition senators) who would conduct the "investigation" and judge the President based on the evidence contained in the seven boxes of evidence – and more. If the disquieting plan of things would be followed, then Pres. Arroyo is finished!

Then the "Hello, Garci" generals would not like to be left in the lurch, so to speak! No wonder, there is more than a flame of unease in the top military echelon of the Armed Forces of the Philippines.

117

View 30

The Darkened Transparency

The now "cancelled" ZTE Philippine-Chinese scandalous contract is still manifesting some lingering and collateral damage to the image of the Arroyo Administration. What a beaten-down scandal of kickbacks in high places of government.

When the ZTE broadband scandal is still at its formative stage, Malacanang alleges that the Palace has conducted a "quiet" internal investigation and it proudly announces that "there was no bribe" that took place. Then later, Pres. Arroyo herself admits that in fact there is an offer of bribe to NEDA Director-General Romulo Neri of P200 million by then Commission of Elections Chairman Benjamin Abalos. Reacting to this irregular situation, Makati Mayor Jejomar C. Binay, comments: "The conflicting reports are characteristic of the flip-flop and double-talk of this (Pres. Arroyo) administration."

In the meanwhile, acting NEDA Director-General Augusto Santos refuses to turn over to the Senate all ZTE-related documents by invoking that the pertinent documents are covered by Pres. Arroyo's "executive privilege." Interestingly enough, there is a nagging contention that Pres. Arroyo herself first approves, later disapproves, then approves the ZTE contract. Under this circumstance, it is extremely difficult to engage in scenario-problem strategy in pinpointing the truth. Definitely, there is a blip in the supposedly "honest" trajectory of corruption-larded administration of Pres. Arroyo.

Santos asserts that the discussions during the NEDA-Investment Coordinating Committee (ICC) conference in which Senate investigators are interested are "covered by executive privilege" and could not, therefore, be divulged publicly, even in a congressional inquiry!

Santos further asserts that "the discussion is a closed-door Cabinet and NEDA meetings which are considered to fall under executive privilege and necessarily, the minutes of said closed-door meetings are also covered by executive privilege."

To buttress his argument, Santos goes on to say: "Further, the NBN project is not yet a finalized project and it is therefore premature to release documents prior to the conclusion of all implementing agreements under the framework of an executive agreement." How can the desire of the Filipino people for the truth if Malacanang, when faced with a congressional inquiry would invoke or at best be animated with "executive privilege hang up." This Arroyo behavior is fast becoming a source of a heavy dose of suspicion that the Arroyo government is guilty of blatant corruption.

On the issue of "executive privilege," Sen. Mar Roxas has the following observations: "I've consulted the lawyers on this. What they say is it has not yet ripened to a so-called 'justifiable' issue. The issues have not been joined, that's why they feel nothing should be brought up to the Supreme Court. But eventually, it will get there. There must be a rejection by the committee on a vote that we reject the invocation, we see the invocation as improper, or the invocation here deals which matters not subject to what executive privilege can legally or properly be applied to. And so therefore once that's joined we now go to the Supreme Court." But, many congressional opposition leaders argue that the Supreme Court is being "used to the hilt" by the President.

As regards the fate of former Comelec Chairman Abalos, it is bruited about widely among the opposition groups that because Pres. Arroyo admits the offer of bribe, Abalos has to be sacrificed in order to contain the damage brought about by the ZTE deal and prevent the "fire from spreading to higher-ups."

On the issue of "executive privilege," Sen. Mar Roxas has the following observations: "I've consulted the lawyers on this. What they say is it has not yet ripened to a so-called 'justifiable' issue. The issues have not been joined, that's why they feel nothing should be brought up to the Supreme Court. But eventually, it will get there. There must be a rejection by the committee on a vote that we reject the invocation, we see the invocation as improper, or the invocation here deals which matters not subject to what executive privilege can legally or properly be applied to. And so therefore once that's joined we now go to the Supreme Court." But, many congressional opposition leaders argue that the Supreme Court is being "used to the hilt" by the President.

As regards the fate of former Comelec Chairman Abalos, it was bruited about widely among the opposition groups that because Pres. Arroyo admitted the offer of bribe, Abalos had to be sacrificed in order to contain the damage brought about by the ZTE deal and prevent the "fire from spreading to higher-ups."

On another front, Speaker de Venecia in October 2007 expresses grave concern on the validity of the "impeachment" initiative by Ruel Pulido, a supposed lackey of Pres. Arroyo. The impeachment move has been endorsed posthaste by Laguna Rep. Edgar San Luis, whose understanding of the purpose of the impeachment remains most elusive. He seems not to understand its purpose, and without purpose, understanding is frivolous and futile.

Hence, House Speaker De Venecia shares his doubts that he would transmit without delay the impeachment complaint which many characterized as bogus. The Pangasinan powerful solon adds: "I already had this investigated (on October 9, 2007), and if the minority congressmen's claims of their having been offered a bribe by Kabalikat ng Malayang Pilipino (Kampi) deputy secretary general, lawyer Francis Ver, that would really be bad. It will be as if we (in the House of Representatives) are being taken for fools. It will be difficult to us to endorse this impeachment complaint if this has been paid for with bribes." Just exactly what do we have here? A political ally of Pres. Arroyo in the House, now turning a critic of the administration! Can we charge this De Venecia transformation to his son's (De Venecia III's) involvement in the ZTE scandal in which the name of the First Gentleman, Miguel Arroyo is being linked?

Do we see here the making of a political orgy?

View 31

The President's Moral Compass Is Screwed Up

I don't know what's wrong with Pres. Arroyo's moral compass. She is again involved in a moral malfunction. Is she that dense that she is unable to distinguish between "bribe" and "donation?" What a "weak-kneed" justification as to why she gives cash to190 congressmen and provincial governors after she talks to them in the Palace. As a matter of fact, even her own kitchen cabinet members do not know how to brush aside the highly immoral act of a woman who is obsessed with power.

Is the stash of cash in the amounts ranging from P200,000 to P500,000 a "Christmas Gift?" Or it is a "donation" borne out of Pres. Arroyo's abiding sense of magnificence and philanthropy? Or is it pure, unadulterated, on-your-face bribery?

If you don't know the answer, well you are not alone. Just consider what her Executive Secretary Eduardo Ermita blurts out when asked about the reported cash distribution in the Palace, particularly the bundle of crisp pesos. His terse comment: "I wasn't present during the governors' meeting."

"I don't care where the money came from as long as it is meant for a good cause.," Press Secretary Bunye says. Good for whom? Good for what?

Other Arroyo Palace subalterns feign ignorance of the entire sordid bribery scandal.

And this brings us to the military. When the military, even a small segment of it, starts to manifest some convulsive reactions to the bribery, the stability of the Arroyo government is placed in jeopardy. She seems to have the flair of provoking the wrath of some officers and men in uniform. The lady Commander-in-chief appears to develop a formula of governance whose grotesque shade inspires nothing but disgust and abhorrence.

Maj. Gen. Dolorfino always emphasizes the importance of remaining neutral. He also instills in his men respect of the Constitution and adherence to chain of command. There is a strong possibility of civil war in which the military will have a significant role. However, Gen. Dolorfino observes: "this possibility (of military coup) cannot be discounted." In the one remaining bastion of reason, Dolorfino adds: "We should be neutral because we are the only institution that is entrusted by the society to maintain peace and order... If there are other groups who will sow violence in our country, there is an organization where they can lodge their trust...."

The general continues: "If the Armed Forces joins, there is no other group that will benefit from it but the enemies of the state, the CPP/NPA, the rebel groups, the terrorist groups, the organized crime groups. And it is not far-fetched that there is going to be civil war if the Armed Forces of the Philippines will be involved."

Sounding like the impending twitched of a banjo, this Arroyo administration seems to be at the throes of a political meltdown.

View 32

Inside The Malacanang Palace

The following excerpts from my book: A CALL FOR REAL DEMOCRAY, in which I include my letters to Pres. Gloria Macapagal Arroyo. My first letter mentions my recollections of my stay in Malacanang in 1986 when I served as the Political Analyst at the Office of the President (Corazon Aquino):

"I am yet to write a first-account book about the first critical months and year of President Aquino's government. At this juncture, I would like to share with you the following:

l. Malacanang Palace then was virtually a "beleaguered military fortress" when nearly every evening security "red alerts" are nightly occurrence. Why? Because:

a. PSG contingents composed of the Marines, Navy, Army and others, are essentially "unhappy" of their treatment by Pres. Aquino's Palace lieutenants and advisers.

b. They view, rightly or wrongly, that some of the top advisers of the President are "leftists" and "Communist sympathizers." Among them, Joker Arroyo, Rene Saguisag, Sanchez, among others. Sanchez who is appointed Secretary of Labor, but whose appointment is withdrawn due to national and international business and industry pressures.

c. At least two (2) nights I could remember when the entire Presidential Security Command troops "abandon" the presidential Palace. They cross the Pasig River to go to their main Headquarters. Pres. Aquino is viewed by these military PSG troopers as NOT the president of our country. (They share with me their frustrations and suspicion). No wonder there are several military coup attempts, which the media places at eight (8). This I know because all tell me every morning of the incident or occurrence the previous night. In one of these military coup attempts under the leadership of Col. Gregorio" Gringo" Honasan, a former senator and now in a military prison on suspicion that he was the alleged "brain" of the Magdalo Oakwood military mutiny in 2003, Malacanang is nearly overtaken. In that incident Noy Noy Aquino, son of then President Corazon C. Aquino, who is running for the Senate in May 2007, is shot supposedly by the rebel troops as reported by the media the following day.

d. Madam President, I must now tell you and the Filipino people that Noy Noy, was NOT shot by the rebel troops of Col. Honasan. The bullets came from the Palace! Go figure it.

I will tell you also something about one of the possible reasons (and this is only my conjecture) why Pres. Aquino did not get the much-coveted Nobel Peace Prize award. As a Political Analyst in the Palace, I had to attend meetings held by different embassies in Manila. My counterparts in these embassies would call me to request for my political analyses. I told them my "frank" opinions. So again figure it out why Pres. Aquino, at the last minute failed to receive the Nobel Peace Prize award! In its stead, a president of a

Central American country with no known spectacular achievements in peace initiatives receives the Nobel Peace Prize. Incidentally, does the name of Gen. Ramon Montano ring a bell to you now? He is one of the top generals of President Aquino who has some say in the deployment of military units as Palace security forces? Figure that one, too.

Incidentally, you may wish to know why all are telling me all those security glitches and breaches. You see, Madam President, practically every morning when I buy my breakfast outside the Palace, I would bring some Tagsilog, Tapalog (fried egg with meat), etc., for these PSG troopers at the gate for their breakfast. Can you imagine the Aquino government is only allocating P12 daily food allowance! Jun Manalili and I would prepare coffee and crackers or bread for some PSG army troopers who would be asked to provide security to the Palace every night when there are "red alerts." They knew that they have something to eat in our Room. Some in full battle gears and heavily armed to their teeth would sleep in the hallways outside our Ministry of Political Affairs office.

2. Part of my responsibility as a Political Analyst is to feel the pulse of the people about the Aquino government. I work and collaborate with. Teddy Benigno who is then the Malacanang Press secretary. Prior to his appointment he is the head of the Agence France Presse in our county. He assign Joel Paredes to cover extensively my hunger strike at Paco Church (re Tatalon squatter killings by the PSG troops of then Pres. Marcos). Once he visits me at Paco Church door steps where I am conducting my hunger protest.

3. Then, I was invited to be the guest speaker of the Rotary Club in one of their meetings at the Club Filipino, in San Juan. I ask them after my short comments to compare corruption during the Marcos era and the Aquino

government. I am shocked to learn from these businessmen that corruption "actually tripled or even quadrupled" during the Aquino rule since many government officials "are now asking for grease money." During Marcos time, only the President's sycophants, Imelda's trusted confidants but equally rapacious ala-lay along with General Ver's die-hard Ilocos military tuta (lap dog), are the only ones demanding bribes. Under Pres. Aquino ALL seem 'gutom' (hungry) and demanding bribe! Does the name Peping Cojuangco ring a bell or whistle to you? Or her brother-in-law? Go figure it that one, too, Madame President.

4. On top of this, there are more extra-judicial killings, too. Also "salvaging" seems to become "fashionable" at the few months of the Aquino government.

5. I knew then I would quit my job at the Palace. Then Atty. Rene Saguisag, one of the top advisers of the President, in one of palace press conferences or briefings says that "corruption is here to stay."

Must he need to say that? I know I had to resign by announcing it the following morning outside the Palace gate. I carried a big placard. The media knows about it since Saguisag invites me through some newsmen to have a meeting with him in his office inside Malacanang. One of the newsmen is Joel Paredes. I politely turn down the invitation and continue my one-day demonstration to express my disappointment with Pres. Aquino's govern-ment. The media did not shine to it perhaps because people are still enamored by President Aquino shortly after the emotional wash of the People Power. Only Daniel J. Hernandez of then Midday afternoon newspaper front pages it describing my act as one by a "crusader." Soon thereafter I leave for the United States.

View 33

After Ex-Pres. Joseph Estrada's Pardon

Recently pardoned ex-Pres. Estrada dares Pres. Arroyo to revoke the pardon. Why is he huffing mad? The resentment of Estrada could not be considered a slow-burn beef of a gripe against Pres. Arroyo. In a DzMM radio interview, Estrada declares that he "will fight to the death" if the Sandiganbayan will seize his personal assets, in addition to the earlier identified wealth that are ruled by the court to be subject to government forfeiture, such as the Boracay Mansion, the funds of the Erap Muslim Youth Foundation and the Jose Velarde bank account. Estrada claims that the government could forfeit them since these were never his properties and assets to begin with. However, he is most adamant and firm in putting a fight against the government in the forfeiture of his lawfully acquired properties and assets that have nothing to do with the alleged ill-gotten wealth which is supposedly amassed and illegally stashed during his presidency.

"Modesty aside, my family is quite well-off...my grandmother has an ancestral home in Laguna. We had the biggest house, a mansion when we transferred to San Juan. I ruled through service and not greed. If I stole the people's money, I would not have the face to appear before the public. That is why I am fighting" the Arroyo government now. Frankly, one can consider such statement an amazingly fluent nuts and bolts hurrah of self-righteousness!

Can Pres. Arroyo constitutionally revoke the Estrada pardon? Not so, according to Sen. Miriam Defensor-Santiago, a former Constitutional professor at the University of the Philippine and a trial judge before becoming a senator. Sen. Santiago describes the possibility of the revocation of the pardon as "next to impossible." Pres. Arroyo can no longer take back the pardon or even declare it null and void even if a violation is committed because it is an "unconditional one."

Sen. Santiago adds: "I am only trusting what I read in the papers. If it is accurately reported as having been 'full, complete and absolute pardon,' then the mere fact that he has violated the law will, of course, incur liability in the prosecution service for him, but it will not necessarily lift the pardon." However, the lady senator surmises that "if the person pardoned violates the conditions of his pardon it becomes null and void." However this does not appear to be applicable to Estrada's case since the pardon signed by Pres. Arroyo is "unconditional."

An interesting footnote: The Boracay Mansion in New Manila, Quezon City, which the government has forfeited is according to Estrada was not his own. It is reported earlier that it is a mansion used as a trysting nest he gives to one of his paramours while he is president. On November 17, it has been reported that the Sandiganbayan receives checks amounting to P215 million from Banco de Oro. Said amount is from the account of the Erap Muslim Youth Foundation. More millions are expected to come. Now who says being president is not a "lucrative" business!

Dennis Villa-Ignacio, the Chief government prosecutor who strongly recommends that Estrada should not have been pardoned threatens to resign if the full forfeiture of identified ill gotten wealth would not be made. This Estrada pardon remains a front burner political issue, especially with Estrada now literally strutting his political stuff (as a "poor man who cares for the poor" merrily going around in places like Payatas, Smokey Mountains, and other pockets of poverty in Metro Manila, giving free food stuffs).

Another interesting note: When the budding politician Estrada runs for mayor of San Juan, he depicts himself as "a poor man, for the masses." Now he boasts that his family is supposedly a landed family. A rich family. That he is not a poor man, a common man, who eats with his hands. Many of Estrada's critics, who strongly oppose his pardon accuse him, even while he is still in office, as mayor of San Juan, Senator, Vice-President and President as a virtually a "hoofed political locust of hypocrisy."

View 34

Forgiveness Good For The Soul

On August 22, 2007, 12 Magdalo military officers are found guilty of violating Articles of War 96 or conduct unbecoming an officer and a gentleman. Brig Gen. Nathaniel Legaspi, president of the seven-man General Court Martial declares: "The 12 officers brought a great dishonor to the noble profession of arms."

The military judgment would have to be approved by Pres. Arroyo who serves as the Commander-in-Chief of the Armed Forces of the Philippines (AFP). Since they are to be separated from the military service dishonorably, they would all forfeit their salaries, allowances and other benefits accorded to the junior officers. Sen. Trillanes is supposed to be the leader of the Oakwood mutineers in February 2003 demanding the resignation of Pres. Arroyo, National Defense Secretary, Gen. Angelo Reyes and Gen. Victor Corpuz, the head of the Intelligence Service of the Armed Forces of the Philippines (ISAF). Only Gen. Corpuz left the service as a result of said upheaval. Gen. Reyes is still much on the saddle! He has become the Teflon cabinet member of the Arroyo Administration. Reyes is the most recycled current cabinet member of the Arroyo government. Why? Pres. Arroyo is extremely grateful to Reyes since he helps to catapult her to the presidency in a most unconstitutional manner in 2001. The military mutineers charge Pres. Arroyo of corruption and demand that she step down. Later, they peacefully surrender. Now the ultimate fate of the 12 officers depends on the final decision of Pres. Arroyo (184 enlisted men who participated in the mutiny are jailed for two years and would be allowed to rejoin the military).

View 35

The Display Of Gestapo-Like Behavior

Mayor of Makati City, Jejomar Binay, is ordered "suspended!"

Imagine the Arroyo administration for reasons only known to it, displays a Gestapo-like pattern of behaviors. Ah, what a show of arrogance of power! And it comes like a political thunderbolt. Unexpected. If the motive is to quash the opposition's chance of victory in May 14, then it just backfired for Pres. Arroyo.

Why would the Ombudsman in cahoots with the Department of Interior and Local Government (DILG) move nearly clandestinely in serving the order of suspension late Friday (May 4) night to Mayor Binay, the United Opposition president. The timing is forebodingly disquieting. It sends a chilling message to those who oppose the Arroyo government that they will be punished if they do so. Pres. Arroyo seems to be sending a clear-eyed message: "Criticize me at your own risk!" What a polity of intimidation which seems to operate essentially with undemocratic stirrings!

In serving the order of suspension, there was a police "siege" of Makati City Hall. It was really unnecessary. They could have served the "order" during the regular office hours. Why in late Friday evening? So that Mayor Binay would be denied of his ability to contact his lawyer, Rene Saguisag, to make the necessary legal steps. The courts are closed on a weekend. With this legal tactic, Mayor Binay had to be in jail during the weekend! Where is the scale of moral values of the Arroyo administration?

Leading Filipino legal eagles contend that the Ombudsman/DILG action is legally flawed. It is a recycle of a dismissed charges filed by a bitter political opponent of Binay who never wins an elective position in Makati.

The Ombudsman solely handles anti-graft complaints. But charges against Binay was a "purely administrative" matter, and that no government personnel can be hired or fired during election time, as the law provides.

Another government tactic being employed in the case of Makati. The suspension order comes just a few days after the Bureau of Internal Revenue orders the garnishment of the properties of Makati for supposedly unpaid taxes.

Poor Gloria, she is sinking deeper and deeper in the quagmire of anti-Arroyo sentiments howling and spanning throughout the country. The May 14 election is a loud-out and clear referendum on the Pres. Arroyo. She knows it, her TU candidates know it, their mother-in-laws know it, their neighbors know it, and even the Neanderthals of Mt. Makiling know it.

Many political candidates of the Arroyo administration are running like nervous ninnies. After May 14 election, many of them will pass out of sight. So much the better for the country. Why, even the head honcho of the "king maker of the Arroyo Club" Speaker Jose de Venecia, Jr. is running scared – not on empty, His rival congressional candidate, Benjie Lim, the mayor of Dagupan City, is putting a good fight. Who knows he might yet earn the "David and Goliath" medal for slaying the giant of the Pangasinan politics. De Venecia is a staunch, die-hard and in-your-face supporter of Pres. Arroyo.

Consider the "raid" of the Makati City Hall just to serve the Order of Suspension: Hundreds of police from the National Capital Region Police Command, the Philippine

National Police Regional Special Action Unit (RSAU) and Southern Police District, reportedly led by Senior Supt. Calunsad, surround the city hall, securing the ground floor and disarming the security personnel of Mayor Binay. Poor kababayans. It would probably take more than a year to catch their breath to recover from this dictatorial show of force. No wonder, Mayor Binay cries: "Makati is under de facto martial law."

Rep. Liza Maza of the Gabriela declares that Pres. Arroyo is getting desperate as the election nears, as seen from the sloppy attempt to eliminate the opposition as exemplified by the unlawful issuance of suspension order against Binay. As if Malacanang is concerned, the May 2007 election is all about saving its queen, Pres. Arroyo. They will lie, cheat, bamboozle the law and justice system so as to assure that she clings to power.

And it is heard around the office coolers the morning after the Makati "siege" that "Malacanang is distancing from the controversial suspension of Mayor Binay." Malacanang Presidential Legal Counsel Apostol, says that "It's Binay's fault. Maybe Bureau of Internal Revenue Commissioner Mario Bunag was already fed up with him, on his refusal to settle obligations the reason a suspension order was slapped on him."

Apostol continues: "We (Pres. Arroyo administration) have nothing to do with it. It's Binay's fault. Now he cries political persecution and that we are behind this move. Why should we be blamed for his lapses?" What a flirtatious assertion of nonsense!

Political Affairs Adviser of Pres. Arroyo loudly snorts: "Ms. Arroyo is innocent of the allegation being made by Binay...Nobody in Malacanang even knew about the suspension order until it had been issued," Yeah, right! If you believe that then Grand Canyon is just like as "isang lubak sa Roxas Boulevard." (only a mere chuckhole in Roxas Boulevard).

The GO (opposition candidates, especially the senatorial bets) will go for the victory next week. Unless of course if Pres. Arroyo will cheat, as she did in May 2004. If she did it before and it appears she is getting away from it, what will prevent her from cheating again. If she does, well, the country could bristle with a new wave of demand for her to resign, if not, the Filipino people could stage a widespread open revolt, this time, it could be very well succeed in having in our country a regime change.

View 36

Supreme Court And The Extra-Judicial Killings

More than a sliver of concern, the Supreme Court instructs the Court of Appeals to provide it with an inventory of extra-judicial killing cases. This latest attempt to determine the causes of the slaying of many human rights workers and leaders, opposition politicians and their followers, lawyers and journalists rippled through our highest court.

In an attempt to have a legal framework, Supreme Court Chief Justice Reynato Puno demands from the Court of Appeals Presiding Justice Ruben Reyes to conduct an inventory of such cases and then submit a report of its findings with the end in view to having a "speedy disposition." This is obviously an attempt by the Arroyo government which is besieged in the international circle of nations and human right organizations to project a positive international image.

The final report of UN Human Rights Commission rapporteur Philip Alston, who investigates the extra-judicial slayings in the Philippines in February 2007 has yet to be released. But it is widely speculated that the Alston UN final report has been leaked. In that findings, Alston recommends that the court should take an aggressive stance to curb these killings by ordering the speedy prosecutions of those "security forces" charged of human rights violations. It is, therefore, an effort by the Arroyo administration to fly on the wings of international denunciation that her government is not aggressive enough in putting a stop to these extra-judicial killings.

The Supreme Court chief declares that he issues the order in response to the observation that numerous cases involving killings of political activists and members of the media have been filed and pending before the various courts in the country.

It is now clear that the Arroyo government is having difficulty navigating the choppy waters of national and international negative attention and denunciations.

In late March 2007, it has been reported that the Inter-Parliamentary Union (IPU) is sending a fact-finding mission to the Philippines on April.18. Not too long ago, Bishop Beverly Shamana, head of a 16-member United Methodist Church of the United States California-Nevada Conference, which investigates the extra-judicial killings in the Philippines recently issues a statement after their investiga-tion: "We will urge US Senators and Congressmen to withdraw support for the Arroyo administration of US government until the series of political assassinations in the country is resolved."

Philip Alston observes that the "Philippine military remains in state of almost total denial of its need to respond effectively and authentically to the significant number of killings attributed to it."

The International News Safety Institute (INSI) expresses grave concern over the assassination of members of the Philippine media.

Puno warns the judges of the trial courts throughout the country that failure to submit such inventory would be a ground for withholding the salaries and allowances of the judges, clerks of court and branch clerks of court concerned "without prejudice to whatever administrative sanction the SC may impose on them."

It comes to the attention of the Chief Justice that an earlier set-up to try these heinous crimes has been scuttled since even those judges involved are themselves being the targets of assassination.

In the current SC plan, there would be three special courts each in Manila, Quezon City, and Makati City and two each in the cities of Pasay, Caloocan and Pasig.

Under the SC guidelines, the special courts may determine whether the crime is a "political killing" by considering the political affiliation of the victim, method of attack, as well as reports that state agents were involved in the commission of the crime. The SC orders continuous trial of such cases, which shall be terminated within 60 days from commencement of the hearing.

Why this sudden interest of the Philippine Supreme Court in the extra-judicial slayings in the country? It appears that the Arroyo administration is under international pressures to take some tangible and visible steps to project a positive image to the critics, especially to the leaders of international human rights organizations.

Several international organizations are gearing up in investigating these assassinations. Alston is scheduled to submit his findings to the United Nations Human Rights Council (UNHRC). He is expected to reveal his findings highly critical of Pres. Arroyo's government, in a speech he would be making before the 4th session of the UNHRC to be held in Geneva, Switzerland in mid-April 2007.

Senator Sharon Costairs of Canada and IPU Secretary General Anders Johnsson may join the fact-finding team. It has also been reported that the European Commission (EC), along with executive body of the European Union (EU) is contemplating sending its own investigating team to the Philippines soon. The US State Department is also sending a fact-finding team.

Due to this development, the slow-creeping wheels of justice insofar as the extra-judicial assassinations are concerned would have to move faster this time. The Arroyo can no longer afford to move in halting or faltering manner since the world community has finally taken cognizance of the disturbing human rights violations in the Philippines.

View 37

The President Who Dares To Be Impeached On ZTE Scandal

One would recall that Pres. Arroyo nearly two years ago dares the opposition members of the House of Representatives: "Impeach me!" They did twice and twice the attempts to impeach her fizzled out. That is when there is a political honeymoon between Malacanang and the House of Representatives.

But why would she do it again this time particularly in the wake of the ZTE NBN scandalous contract? This time, Malacanang is stage-managing this highly questionable move to "impeach her." Anakpawis party-list Rep. Crispin Beltran reveals in a privileged speech on the floor that a Malacanang "messenger," an emissary with a pocket-full of grease money offers "2 million for him to endorse the impeachment complaint, which has been filed clandestinely on October 7, 2007. Congressman Dan Fernandez of Laguna, an ardent critic of the administration reveals that he too has been approached by a Malacanang "messenger" and offers him a "lump sum" if he would sign the new impeachment complaint.

This disturbing revelation comes about when Makati Rep. Teodoro Locsin exposes this "frivolous impeachment complaint." against Pres. Arroyo. In the plenary deliberation in the Lower House, he accuses Rep. San Luis of not knowing exactly what he is endorsing. The Makati solon also lambasts San Luis for his inability to follow House protocol. The "new impeachment complaint" should have been referred to the House Committee on Good Government instead of the House Committee on Justice.

When further grilled by Locsin to provide an elucidation on the merit of the impeachment filed on October 7, San Luis offers the following lame excuse: "I cannot debate with the honorable Congressman from Makati who had studied in Harvard as I only studied in the University of Sto. Tomas." The heated verbal exchange was triggered when the Makati representative tries to get some answers as to why San Luis is supporting the bogus impeachment complaint despite of its blatantly obvious "infirmities." Rep. Ronaldo Zamora, a House Minority Leader, emphasizes such sham impeachment drive has only one purpose: to afford Pres. Arroyo an immunity for at least one more year when a real and viable impeachment complaint could be filed against the president.

But why would this new "impeachment complaint" being initiated by San Luis a member of Pres. Arroyo's Kampi party, is considered highly questionable? It is a sham, a spurious attempt to insulate Pres. Arroyo from being removed through a meritorious, well-grounded and justifiable impeachment at some appropriate time. File spurious "impeachment" now and any attempt to remove her through real impeachment would have to wait for another year. That's why.

There is another political trajectory involved here. Rep. Roilo Golez claims: "The minority is not inclined to support this since this (new impeachment initiative) appears to be a majority matter, an internecine war in the making." Another opposition congressman offers his take on the issue: "This plot is obviously centered on retribution against the Speaker after his son implicates the First Gentleman in the national broadband project cornered by China's ZTE Corp. The most logical way of getting even with the Speaker is to oust him." Oh my, there seems to be fire in the bellies of both Pres. Arroyo and House Speaker De Venecia in this free-for-all-matira-matibay (let the fittest survive) political melee!

View 38

Flip-Flopping All The Way

There must be an excess of Christmas spirit in Malacanang Palace or what?

Remember former Congressman Romeo Jalosjos? He was convicted of statutory rape many years ago. Recently he was supposed to have been "pardoned" by Pres. Arroyo only to be sent back to Muntinlupa National Bilibid Prison!

Who is responsible for this latest administration snafu? "I am faulting her (Pres. Arroyo)" Sen. Richard Gordon says. Then he pointedly asks: "Are pardons only for presidents? Are pardons only for the rich? That should not be the standard taken in the grant of presidential pardon." He insists that it is the pardon of former Pres. Estrada that sets the stage for the release of Jaloslos from prison.

Upon hearing Sen. Gordon's verbal thrashing, Sen. Jinggoy, who is currently the Senate President Pro Tempore, quickly lashes back saying that his father's case should not be equated with former Rep. Jaloslos "pardon." He underscores that while the convictions for both his father and former solon are criminal in nature, "my father was not guilty of rape…that his conviction was a political one."

Sen. Miriam Defensor Santiago, another political ally of Pres. Arroyo in the Senate characterizes Jaloslos' pardon as "cruel, bizarre joke." The crusty, feisty senator wonders aloud: "The issue is where did these documents come from…If the President said she did not authorize it, then who authorized those documents?"

Now the Arroyo administration is moving heaven and earth in trying hard to wiggle out of the "bizarre" and "cruel" joke?

View 39

My Thanksgiving Thought

This week we celebrate Thanksgiving. For me it has special meaning. Beautiful and enduring significance. In our adopted country, America, we enjoy the full blessing of democracy. The ability to express our sentiments. The opportunity to bring to light some dark sides of life. Not that I am perfect. Far from it. But at least we can expose widespread government corruption without being slapped with libel in court and be threatened to be sent to jail; without being arrested or salvaged by some government military or police elements or paramilitary agents if we become more vocal and articulate in expressing our concerns, hurts and grievances.

Imagine if we who are fortunate to be in a position to acquit ourselves this responsibility decide to keep quiet. To hush up. To ultimately become a part of our collective political memory's endpoint of castrated sense of responsibility. What if we settle and accept the fact of being slammed into uncaring obscurity? What if we just fold our hands and accept being obliterated into our own very existence of obstinacy amid massive government malfeasance?

What if we just look the other way when our country is in the quagmire of political chicanery? What if the considerable swatch of government officials in higher places who are more than piranhas who remain unchallenged in their nesting territorial zone of abuse of authority and power are not exposed? Are we to remain in the sinkhole of indifference? Personally, I would consider it an asphyxiation not only of my being but of my moral values. Not that I am a saint. I am a sinner more than I can say. But I have at least the compunction to admit it.

Today, let me count my ways in lifting myself a little bit higher behind the passionate edge of Thanksgiving:

1. Thanks for allowing me in April 2005, to have the courage and guts to carry a placard at the foot of the Ninoy Aquino's monument in Ayala Avenue in Makati stating: "IT IS NOT THE CHA CHA, BUT THE HELLO GARCI CHEATING, STUPID!"

2. Thanks for allowing me to literally make my blood boil over the attempts to impeach Pres. Gloria Macapagal-Arroyo for three times only to be stymied repeatedly by Malacanang unchecked, blatant and vulgar bribery, i.e., consider the latest P500,000 cash "gift" contained in brown paper bags given to 190 congressmen and local officials in the confines of the Presidential Palace recently. Oh my, oh my. The political barbarians are no longer knocking on the gate of the palace, but they are already inside the palace!

3. Thanks for allowing me to jump down the throats of many named Filipino politicians for their alleged participation in graft-tainted ZTE National Broadband scandal which involved more than US $329 million; North Rail Project caper, the Joc-Joc Bolante Fertilizer scandal in which congressmen from districts without farms received Malacanang Fund; the Diosdado Macapagal Highway (the most

expensive abbreviated, stunted and pint-sized highway in the world smacked in the heart of Luneta Park; Jose Pidal scandal; to mention a few.

4. Thanks for the opportunity to write a book which chronicles the sins of Pres. Arroyo's government, entitled: THE RISE AND DECLINE OF PRESIDENT GLORIA MACAPAGAL-ARROYO. (Order on line: AMAZON.COM).

Addison, a famous philosopher once said: "Charity is a virtue of the heart, and not of the hands." Not allowing cunning to be taken as sinister, I would like to paraphrase Addison: "In Philippine politics, charity is virtue of dirty hands and deep pockets."

View 40

Ungrateful Or What?

The newly pardoned former Pres. Estrada is now being accused by many political pundits and followers of caving in to the wishes of Malacanang since he is eternally grateful for the unconditional pardon he receives from Pres. Arroyo. That many fear that Estrada could end up as a political bogeyman of the Arroyo administration; that the former mayor of San Juan who rises to the presidency of our country only to end up in disgrace and ignominy needs to reexamine his political value; that it needs the much needed political tune up because of his perceived political somersault.

But then Estrada immediately douses off the accusations. He has been quoted: "I still remain an opposition" as long as the Philippines is under the leadership of Pres. Arroyo. He reiterates that he will continue to be in the opposition corner until a "new and true leader whose genuine concern is for the masses is found."

Just because he accepts an "unconditional and absolute pardon" from Pres. Arroyo mean that he would abandon the bravura and raucous spirit of the opposition.

There is no limited reservoir of opposition leaders who defend the pardoned president. The Minority Leader in the Senate, Sen. Aquilino Pimentel Jr. underscores the fact that because Estrada accepted the executive clemency, it does not mean that he surrenders his belief of the illegitimacy of Pres. Arroyo's presidency. That Erap still questions the utter lack of demonstrable legitimacy of the Arroyo administration. Sen. Manuel Villar, the Senate President, joins Sen. Pimentel in assuring that ex-president Estrada's unconditional pardon will not "dampen" the resolve of the opposition to continue "exposing and checking the misuse of power and corrupt ways of the Arroyo government."

Amid the welter of fretful skepticism of the former president's political commitment to remain a fiscalizer, his son, San Juan Mayor Joseph Victor Ejercito assures that his father will "never" become an ally of the president and that he will never accept any position, exalted or not, in the Arroyo administration.

The question in the mind of the people: Will Erap become the titular head of the opposition? United Opposition president Makati Mayor Binay comments that it would be premature to come to that conclusion. At the present time, such speculation remains in the rarefield of political moments of speculation.

The timing of the unconditional pardon is worthy of picking the nits off its worth and rationale. Why? It comes at a time when Pres. Arroyo's administration is mired in scandals, i.e., ZTE, Joc Joc Bolante Fertilizer scandal, the "Hello, Garci" controversy, among others. However, at least two religious groups express support of the presidential clemency. El Shaddai leader Bro. Mike Velarde and Iglesia ni Kristo Spokesman Bro. Bienvenido Santiago write the lady Chief Executive that "the pardon will significantly help in promoting national unity and political stability that our country and people badly need to improve our economic and security conditions. We hope and pray that our national leaders will take your action as a positive step toward national healing and reconciliation and join hands to move our country forward." To the many top-notch legal minds of the country, such pardon done with some indecent haste is reason for them to fall in disquietude.

View 41

Who's Afraid Of Erap?

Pres. Arroyo, that's who! May 2010 may still be a long way to go for our people to have a new president. But even this early, the Nacionalista Party is dangling the name of Senate Pres. Manuel Villar; the Liberal Party is vetting Sen. Mar Roxas. And then there is a mushrooming of other high visibility opposition leaders who are gunning for the presidency, i.e., Sen. Panfilo Lacson, Mayor of Makati City Jejomar Binay, Sen. Loren Legarda, Sen. Richard Gordon, among others. One politician, Davao City Representative Nograles even surmises that Sen. Jinggoy Estrada could be a "good" presidential bet.

And then lately, the name of former Pres. Estrada is being mentioned prominently. Like an unwelcome weed cropping up from an abandoned concrete road, there is a growing public clamor for convicted president to run for president in May 2010.

Not possible, according to Pres. Arroyo. She is so worried that Estrada could sweep the opposition candidates to victory in 2010. Through her close adviser, Press Secretary Bunye, she issues a stern warning to Estrada not to even think of running for presidency again. Bunye reveals in the January 3 press briefing that Estrada agrees that should a pardon is extended to him, he would no longer be interested in running in 2010. Bunye underscores: "We can look at the records and they are very clear. They have been disseminated and I recall the former President even signed a copy of that pardon."

Chief Presidential Legal Counsel Apostol chimes in his opinion: "Yes he (Estrada) could oppose the (whereas clause in the pardon, but that would be a ground for us to file a disqualification case against him before the court (Supreme Court)." He then cites the 1987 Constitution which specifically provides that a president who has been elected to the same post before cannot assume the same…" To top it all, Estrada agrees to the pardon with a specific condition that he would no longer be interested in running for the presidency. Naturally, the legal eagles and political gurus of the Estrada camp argue that should the former San Juan mayor decide to run again for the presidency in 2010, he would not be running as a "re-electionist president" since he is not the incumbent president. That Constitutional provision refers to Pres. Arroyo. Not to former Pres. Estrada.

Secretary of Justice Gonzalez shares his legal expertise: "From presidential timbers (down) to presidential toothpicks, all these people (including former Pres. Estrada) want to run." He continues that "being illegally removed as president" does not qualify the popular and charismatic Estrada as one of the candidates in 2010 presidential elections but he adds that "he can still run for other elective posts, except for president. He can run for vice president and other elective positions, but not for president." One wonders why Malacanang is still harboring fear, if not contempt of the possibility of a Estrada run. While he is a convicted plunderer by the Sandiganbayan, Estrada realizes the ego-satisfying element of his political persona. He is an astute individual. He distributes in a breakneck pace free food stuffs everywhere he goes especially in many a squatter and shanty area lately. Estrada plans to continue his free food distribution caravan in the Visayas and Mindanao. What a good slug of showbiz here. Once an actor is always an actor.

View 42

El Loco vs. La Loca

"El loco is el loser..." trumpets the New York Post on December 3, 2007!

However, there is some interesting political footnote to the defeat of Venezuelan President Cesar Chavez's initiatives which our Pres. Gloria Macapagal-Arroyo should take note. The Venezuelan president has been portrayed by many world leaders, particularly by the Pres. George Bush, as a remorseless, if cantankerous, dictator. His behavior is so abrasive and abrading that he earns a reputation as the El Loco of South America. Whereas in our country, many critics and an assorted political detractors and military renegades – captured and still at large – describe our lady president as "La Loca" for power! That La Loca would do anything and everything to be president of our country. She is accused of "stealing" the presidency in 2001 and when her turn to seek her own term in 2004, she "cheated".

Considering the records and outward behavioral manifestations of El Loco in the stage of international politics, Venezuelans were expecting one ugly scenario should Pres. Chavez losses, i.e., the opposition would not be able to evade the scorching political future in an era of super-heated controversy the El Loco has generated in the last few years. He wanted to make Venezuela into a full-fledge "socialist country" like Cuba. As a matter of fact, it seems that Pres. Chavez has adopted Pres. Fidel Castro as his "patron saint" in transforming Venezuela in the image of Cuba. This means that like Castro, Chavez would be the president of Venezuela permanently.

The gracious acceptance of defeat by Pres. Chavez is worthy of praise. It is extraordinary. Unexpected. What is remarkable about this gesture is the graciousness it is done. The Venezuelans and the world observers are pleasantly surprised at the sense of magnanimity he shows after his defeat.

Another political act of Pres. Chavez which puts a shame to the expectation that because of his "dictatorial tendencies" the country would end up pitching from political gloom to diplomatic doom should he lose. It never happens. Pres. Chavez says that his gracious act shows that Venezuela's democracy is "maturing." No more black oil blackmail?

Turn the spotlight to our country. Pres. Arroyo is another kind of leader. While there has been copious dripping military flare-ups she remains stubborn, obstinate and perversely unyielding. In addition, she is vengeful and imbued with an inordinate amount of vindictiveness. Her leadership persona seems to seamlessly blend with dictatorial - cum deceit - tendencies.

Pres. Chavez orders the REFERENDUM thus allowing the Venezuelans to voice their opinion about his policies and governance belief. It is a political risk he takes and when the verdict thumbing down his constitutional initiatives became known, he graciously accepts the decision of the Venezuelan people.

But not Pres. Arroyo. No to Snap Election. No to any kind of Referendum. Nothing to test the will of the Filipino people. We hope the evil of authoritarian leadership does not gather head permanently in our country.

View 43

Display Of Obscene Generosity

Our country is considered one of the most corrupt nations in the world. In Asia, the Philippines is considered second placer. Then Arroyo is tagged as the most corrupt, most sullied and tarnished president in our history. Imagine even worse than the deposed Pres. Ferdinand E. Marcos. This is revealed recently by the Pulse Asia survey. What a crass disregard of morality in public service.

Sparing of words, one can come to a conclusion that there must be money to squander around to divvying up, to dole out among her political allies. Consider the amount of money being given to congressmen and governors lately by the president. Amid the increasing level of poverty in our country, this misplaced generosity is disturbing. It is utterly abhorrent.

Recently, 240 members of Congress each receive P200,000 Christmas bonus. This is revealed by House Speaker Jose De Venecia. He says that his decision is in compliance with Pres. Arroyo's directive. If the money is to benefit the staffs of the congressmen, there would be no quarrel with that. Employees, whether in private sectors and public service, receive Christmas bonuses.

But what is disquieting is the fact that as recent as October 11, more than 150 House members received each P500,000 when they attended a breakfast meeting with Pres. Arroyo. As we know, some provincial governors (including

Pampanga Governor Ed. Panlilio) received in that meeting the same amount of P500,000 each.

If what Speaker De Venecia says that his decision to distribute P200,000 each to members of the House was in accordance with the directive from Malacanang, why then Pres. Arroyo is reported that she is "unhappy" about it. But Malacanang is quick to claim that "it could do nothing about it." Now who exactly is to "blame" for this generous Christmas generosity of heart.

Another display of Malacanang profligacy is demonstrated recently when no less than 34 members of the House of Representatives accompanied Pres. Arroyo in Spain to receive the human rights award, along with the show of extravagance in their visits to France and Great Britain. Does she need 34 Congressmen to tag along in her foreign junkets? What could be the redeeming feature of this presidential foreign visit with a battalion of congressmen and their wives?

Up to the present time, Malacanang is having difficulty explaining where the millions given to House Representatives and some provincial governors come from. Did it come from the pockets of Pres. Arroyo? From Speaker De Venecia? Some avid rah-rah political allies of the president claim that the money comes from the ruling party; some say that it comes from the intelligence funds of the Armed Forces of the Philippines. Some Malacanang lap dogs claim that the money came from the PAGCOR. Certainly, there must be a source. But from where?

I will tell you where. From all of us OFWs remitting more than US$ 15 billion each year! Shakespeare once declares "all the world's stage, and all the men and women merely players." In our country, cabal of corrupt politicians headed by Pres. Arroyo are kingpins of utter corruption. If one feels that we are too harsh in our judgment or observation, just ask your families back home this holiday season. Only lamentation of ordinary Filipinos can be heard. And that the "flow of soul" emanates from poverty of countless Filipino families. Hunger stalks poor families. Countless children go to sleep without eating. Savage beast of hunger leeches away their daily existence. Many of our political leaders display very deep holes in their morality.

View 44

Jalosjos: To Muntinlupa And Back

Remember former Congressman Romeo Jalosjos of Zamboanga? He has been convicted of statutory rape of a minor years ago. Recently he is supposed to have been "pardoned" by Pres. Arroyo, only to be sent back to Muntinlupa National Bilibid Prison later.

Who is responsible for this latest administration snafu? "I am faulting her (Pres. Arroyo)" Sen. Richard Gordon says. Then he continues to ask: "Are pardons only for presidents? Are pardons only for the rich? That should not be the standard taken in the grant of presidential pardon." He insists that it has been the pardon of former Pres. Estrada that sets the stage for the release of Jalosjos from prison.

Upon hearing Sen. Gordon's verbal thrashing, Sen. Jinggoy, who is currently the Senate President Pro Tempore, quickly fires back by saying that his father's case should not be equated with former Rep. Jaloslos' "pardon." He points out that while the convictions for both his father and former solon are criminal in nature, "my father was not guilty of rape...that his conviction was a political one."

Sen. Miriam Defensor Santiago, another political ally of Pres. Arroyo in the Senate characterizes Jaloslos' pardon as "cruel, bizarre joke." The crusty, feisty senator wonders aloud: "The issue is where did these documents come from...If the President said she did not authorize it, then who authorized those documents?" The sniffing out for the truth is in order.

How is the Arroyo administration trying hard to wiggle out of the "bizarre" and "cruel" joke? Simple. Lie to the teeth. Pretend that the Filipino people are stupid, cretinously brainless and idiotic. Take the explanation of that veritable apologist of Pres. Arroyo Secretary of Justice Gonzalez: "The pardon documents as obtained by the media were "merely drafts." Such response by a key Arroyo cabinet member encapsulates wanton waste of logic. It is not only "cruel" but a supplication of mental incongruities, if not bankruptcy.

Sen. Pia Cayetano clearly articulates herself in driving home her concern: "The issue (pardon of Jalosjos) is who authorized the documents...if there were signatures on the documents to the release, then either those signatures were authentic and those who signed are criminally liable... of abuse of authority; or, if the signatures were forged, then it was a public forgery."

Liza Masa of the Gabriela Women's Party claims that Pres. Arroyo gives the pardon but when it is met with repugnance by the public, she withdraws it. Masa accuses Pres. Arroyo's government as a "coddler of rapists."

Jalosjos is now back in Muntinlupa! This fact is underscored by Malacanang Chief Presidential Legal Counsel Apostol: "He (Jalosjos) is still in jail." And then he buttresses his statement: "This is a proof to our critics that we have a listening President who has seen that there is a public clamor to deny him clemency." What a flavorless and "cruel" reasoning were it not salted by bizarreness.

View 45

Arroyo's Venality

More than a handful of justifications, Pres. Arroyo is now considered the "most corrupt president in the Philippine history," as measured by the Pulse Asia (PA) survey conducted very recently. The results of the poll are issued on December 11, 2007.

Sad but true, the Philippines is not only considered to be the most corrupt country in Southeast Asia, but one of the "most corrupt" (out of the top ten) countries in the world, as measured by the Transparency International (TI), a global corruption watchdog.

According to the results of the survey by the TI, the socially and economically well-placed or rich Filipinos view Pres. Arroyo as corrupt with a rating of 50%; the lower and middle class gave her 43% rating; the extremely impoverished or the poor of the poorest gave her a rating of 35%. So what else is new? There seems to be an insatiable appetite for greediness in the government service in our country.

If this is not enough to disturb you, well consider the latest news from Manila. Her political followers in the House of Representatives, especially those who receive brown bags containing P500,000 each are now readying the idea of resurrecting Charter Change (CHA CHA). The last time Pres. Arroyo toys with the idea of CHA CHA, it lurches to nowhere. It literally drown in the under tow of public protests. The Filipino people thumb her down. To some political pundits, some aspects of the CHA CHA deserve public support, but because Pres. Arroyo is behind it, they strongly feel that she is using it to extend her political clawing power beyond 2010.

Rep. Victor Francisco Ortega (1st District, La Union), one of Pres. Arroyo's closest House allies, and chairman of the House committee on constitutional amendments, has recently made overtures to his fellow pro-Arroyo House members as regards the possibility or desirability of re-introducing CHA CHA initiative again!

Rep. Pablo Garcia (2nd District, Cebu), another Arroyo supporter discusses with his House colleagues on how best to revise the Constitution in a way that would cause the "least disturbance to the present system." Garcia comes to an early conclusion that CHA CHA can be undertaken through a Constituent Assembly (CON ASS), Constitutional Convention (CON CON) or through People's Initiative (PI). Pres. Arroyo is amenable to any of these legislative venues.

Of course, all methods have been tried before but all – despite their supposed "lofty" goals – miserably failed. Under Section I, Article 17 of the Constitution, any amendment to, or revision of the Constitution may be proposed by 1) the Congress, upon a vote of three fourths of all its members, or 2) a constitutional convention (CON CON). Now we know why Pres. Arroyo distributes bagful of money (bribes) in Malacanang. Those recipients are now expected to be "dogs in the manger in Malacanang."

View 46

Soon We Will Know

Will there be a reenactment of the "People Power EDSA III" of May 2001 that fizzled out. Recall, if you must, that during the "day of rage" organized by the supporters of then recently ousted Pres. Estrada, they almost reached the gate of Malacanang Palace but they were met with tear-gassing and truncheon-bashing, not to mention the water-cannoning by the national and local police, along with the assistance of the army troopers.

Sometime next month, the Sandiganbayan would issue its decision on the plunder case against detained former Pres. Estrada.

Whatever the result, Pres. Arroyo will find herself in a NO-WIN situation.

In anticipation of possible political flare ups, i.e., people reacting negatively if former Pres. Estrada is convicted, the AFP has announced that it would deploy more than 2,000 troops on the promulgation of Estrada's plunder case in and around Malacanang Palace. There could be mass demonstrations that could march to Palace.

The common wisdom in Philippine politics is that former Pres. Estrada is still considered a veritable political powerhouse. In the May 2007 mid-term election, the former president endorses all the opposition (GO) senatorial candidates. All won, except one, i.e., Juan Miguel Suburi, whose victory is under heavy clouds of suspicion that he lands in the tail end of the 12-senatorial slate through alleged electoral anomalies in counting the Mindanao votes. And if former Pres. Estrada is found NOT GUILTY of plunder, then Pres. Arroyo would find herself being accused of grabbing power and assuming the presidency in 2001 without legitimate reasons. In other words, her ascendancy to the presidency was illegal and unconstitutional. Not allowing brawns to outgun reason, this scenario wherein Pres. Estrada is NOT GUILTY, would be farfetched considering the thirst-quenching itch of the lady executive to stay in power come what may. The "Hello, Garci" caper is a breathtaking example of her propensity to do just that. She is pugnacious to a fault to remain President, legitimately or illegitimately.

And there is another trajectory in which our country could very well find itself orbiting.

Amid the uncertainty surrounding the final verdict by the Sandiganbayan Special Division on the plunder case against Pres. Estrada, there are speculations heard through the grapevine that there could be a military "coup" during this time of political uneasiness. Some disgruntled military officers could fire more than a warning shot across the bow of an increasingly unsettling situation in our country. Reacting to the military coup jitters, Philippine Army commanding general, Lt. Gen. Alexander Yano warns the would-be plotters: "We would take drastic action against troops that would break away."

The military contingency strategy: 2,000 military troops would be assigned to Malacanang Palace at least two day before the Sandiganbayan decision. 6,000 soldiers and police would be deployed in the metropolitan areas.

View 47

Time's Up, Mr. Speaker

The Malacanang wrecking ball, it appears, is starting to swing.

Poor House Speaker De Venecia! It appears the sin of the son is visiting upon the father. Because he fails to dissuade his son De Venecia III aka Joey, from exposing the supposedly scandalous role of the First Couple's in the $329-million ZTE caper, along with the $460-billion Cyber Education contract with China.

Some of the alarming signs against Speaker De Venecia, which could be interpreted as indicating the way of a serpent upon a rock of eventual fall from power. Consider Sen. Juan Ponce Enrile, a staunch supporter of Pres. Arroyo in the Senate, who points the finger of accusation to Speaker De Venecia as the main force behind the controversial $460-million Northrail project, which in Philippine politic, always rakes with huge kickbacks. Did Sen. Enrile get the marching order from Malacanang to start the demolition derby?

And then from the edge of incomprehension, PCGG Chairman Camilo Sabio last week revives the $120-million behest loan case against Speaker De Venecia, a legal matter which had been dropped against the speaker in 1988. In that case, JdV had been accused of failing to pay the $120 million "behest loan" in a compromise agreement.

But before Malacanang and Speaker De Venecia start ripping each other, the Filipinos must be informed of the following scenarios:

1. Speaker JdV can expose and confirm who got a share of the Northrail kickbacks involving million-dollar payoff.
2. He can confirm Sandra Cam's testimony of jueteng payoffs to the Arroyo couple, even before she became president in 2001.
3. He can raise questions on possible kickbacks from the lobbyists of cigarette manufacturers who were successful in reducing the sin tax on their product.
4. He can also ask why the granting of huge VAT exemptions for a Filipino-Chinese tycoon.
5. He also can question why the scandalously overpricing of DPWH infrastructure projects, which could include among others, the British bridges program along with the 35 World Bank contracts.
6. He can also reveal some key information on the use of billions of government funds, i.e., PAGCOR, PCSO, OWWA, PhilHealth and other GOCC funds in the 2004 presidential elections. Money is reportedly used to bribe some top military generals in the infamous "Hello, Garci" wire tap.
7. He can bring out some heretofore details behind the 35 World Bank contracts, along with the 30 other pending project agreements with China which could also include the $5-billion Southrail project.

This PCGG attempt to revive the $120-million behest loan case against Speaker De Venecia could signal woeful times for both Pres. Arroyo and Speaker De Venecia. Imagine if the mudslinging starts thick and heavy. The situation could become frigging bloody. Politically, that is.

View 48

Remember Isabelita Peron?

She became President of Argentina after her husband Juan Peron died.

She was arrested, indicted and found guilty of grave human rights violations. Pres. Arroyo and Pres. Peron share a common reservoir of presidential sin: both are being accused of gross inability to stop summary killings of human rights advocates. Both have touched an obstrusively sensitive, if raw, nerve of the people they govern. Like in the case of Isabelita, Gloria is being widely condemned by international human rights organizations. Because many Filipino journalists had been salvaged or murdered since 2001 when she became President, the Reporters Without Borders condemns her. The United Nations Human Rights Commission and the U. S. Department of State are equally concerned and disturbed with her gross inability to act as the Commander-in-Chief. Certainly there is an erosion on her ability to be an effective leader.

The comparison between Isabelita and Pres. Arroyo is not yet complete. While Isabelita was driven out of power and ultimately sent to exile, Pres. Arroyo's fate is yet to be determined. If the corruption barometer were to be used, i.e., she is "more corrupt" than disgraced Pres. Marcos, then she could face more than exile. She could very well be sent to jail! She would then savor the taste of prison life like what Pres. Estrada endures.

There is a consensus that Pres. Arroyo is being caught asleep at the switch. And it becomes all the more disturbing when her own administration Senate Majority Leader Francis Pangilinan decides to run in the May 2007 senatorial elections as an "independent" rather than be identified with Pres. Arroyo's party. Many observers feel that any support or even the slightest hint of Pres. Arroyo's help could spell political disaster. In the case of Pangilinan, it has been correct. He is now a senator.

All senatorial candidates under her political banner suffer ignominious defeat despite thousands of millions of campaign funds. Says he: "The President holds the key to solving the summary executions of her political critics." The boyish-looking senator continues: "As Commander-in-Chief, Mrs. Arroyo must step in and instruct these generals to come out in the open and speak out about the truth behind the alleged involvement of the military brass in extra-judicial killings. The buck stops with the President as the head of the country's security forces."

Latest reports from Manila indicate that no less than three generals have supposedly implicated the government in the summary executions. If Pres. Arroyo should continue her indifference – during the last remaining three years of her presidency – she and her military generals could find themselves "accountable in the end."

No more political public-relations pratfalls. She should act aggressively. This sound simplistic to say. Why? Many political cognoscenti in our country feel that Pres. Arroyo is actually riding a vicious tiger that she is not now able to dismount fearing that if she attempts to do it, she might find herself in the belly of the tiger (meaning the military generals). What a contemplation of sad scenario currently obtaining in our country.

Back to Isabelita. One will recall that then President of Argentina was accused as being tolerant, if not permissive, of the formation of death squads in Argentina during her presidency that started in 1976. Many critics even accused her of being actually involved in countless summary slayings of her critics. After being found guilty of human rights violations during her incumbency, she sought asylum in Spain. One wonders whether Pres. Arroyo would seek asylum in Hawaii or Guam.

Consider the revelation last weekend by one of the three generals claiming that the summary killings and other extra-judicial slayings of the critics of Pres. Arroyo were "openly" discussed during a top-level military conference about two years ago.

Sen. Pangilinan reminds the President to act now. Otherwise her leadership and her government could capsize and she could find herself suffering the same political fate of Isabelita Peron. In a luminous flash of admonition, Sen. Pangilinan soberly urges Pres. Arroyo to "learn from the painful lessons of history."

View 49

Here Comes The Inter-Parliamentary Union Team

When Pres. Arroyo issues the Presidential Proclamation 1017 in February 2006, the military and the national police had been quick in arresting Party-list congressman Crispin Beltran, among others. At least five of his fellow Party-list congressional colleagues had been threatened with arrest. So they decide to seek safety within the confines of the Batasan Pambansa (House of Representatives) compound.

On April 18, 2007, the Inter-Parliamentary Union's (IPU) three-member fact-finding team arrive in Manila. Their mission: conduct a probe on the spate of extra-judicial killings in the Philippines taking place during Pres. Arroyo's watch.

The IPU team is composed of Sen. Sharon Carstairs (Canada), vice president, IPU committee on Human Rights of Parliamentarians, Anders Johnsson, IPU secretary-general; and Ingborg Schwarz, committee secretary, IPU Committee on Human Rights of Parliamentarians.

Now the seemingly untrammeled pursuit of Party-list "leftists" has finally come to roost. The "Batasan 5" had been ordered arrested by virtue of the Presidential Proclamation 1917. The Arroyo administration seems cottoned to the weird notion that those Party-list" members of the Philippine legislature are behind the destabilization of her government. That since they are considered "leftists" they are a threat to the Republic of the Philippines. That they are all evil-inflicting forces that would topple down the Arroyo citadel of power. This accusation, to many observers, is a political dish being served flat cold. The identified Party-list representatives are as follows: Saturnino "Satur" Ocampo, Teddy Casino and Joel Viador of Bayan Muna; Liza Maza of Gabriela; and Rafael Mariano of Anakpawis. Pay close attention to the organizations they represent. All are identified with the disenfranchised members of our society. Their voices express the collective anguish of a deprived, poor segment of our population. Because of their party affiliations, the Arroyo government has used it as a bully pulpit of irresponsible accusations. In our country, be a poor, or worse be a leader of the poor, and you will experience a wrenching confrontation with the Arroyo government. You will automatically gain the label of "leftist" or supporter of the Communist Party of the Philippines CPP). This Arroyo administration is recklessly schmoozing with nonsense!

And this Arroyo regime will never tire in manufacturing charges so that it can detain and arrest anyone. If you are free, this Arroyo government can charge you whether you are accused of a "crime" that allegedly took place or committed more than 20 years ago! An actual example is the case of Rep. Crispin Beltran of Party-list Anakpawis. He is now in jailed charged with "SEDITION" that took place 20 years ago WHEN SEDITION WAS NOT EVEN IN EXISTENCE! Beltran who is under hospital detention would be interviewed by the IPU members.

IPU Carstairs and Schwarz will preside in the press conference to be held on April 20, at the Sofitel, formerly Westin Philippine Plaza. They will explain the need for such mission and if the findings warrant these charges to be elevated to a higher international body, the team would do so.

It should be remembered that the Geneva-based IPU would hold its annual conference this year in Nusa Dua in Bali on April 29 to May 4, 2007. It is the international body of 144 Parliaments of sovereign nations, which include the Philippines. It appears that this is the "higher" international body that the 3-member IPU delegation is referring. The Union is an international organization which works for peace and cooperation among peoples and for the establishment of representative democracy throughout the world.

The IPU mission would meet with officials of the House of Representatives, Justice Secretary Gonzalez and Chief State Prosecutor Jovencito Zuno, Defense Secretary Hermogenes Ebdane, Interior Secretary Ronaldo Puno, National Security Adviser Norberto Gonzales, the chiefs of the PNP and AFP, Commission on Elections Chairman Benjamin Abalos, Jr. and Commission on Human Right Chair Purificacion Quisumbing.

Recently it has been reported that the European Union (EU) would likely join the representatives of the United States and other countries of Asia, particularly the member-states of the Association of Southeast Asian Nations (ASEAN) in observing the May 14, mid-term elections.

The EU announces that it would send observers in hot spots, where violence and vote rigging usually occur. We hope the grim images of the "Hello, Garci's" blast of the past would not be reenacted in May 2007 mid-term elections.

View 50

A Shameful National Secret

Pres. Arroyo has just come up with a new strategy, equally disgraceful and distasteful.

On September 18, 2007, she informs the Senate, which is investigating the "Hello, Garci" wiretap controversy "to leave the military alone and respect its command structure and disclosure rules." Wow! That's a typical political ju-jitsu only Pres. Arroyo is capable of hatching up when cornered.

But "Hello, Garci" telephone instruction to then Commissioner of Elections Garcillano is about her order to cheat her way to the presidency with "more than one million vote margin."

Last week, Pres. Arroyo intones: "In the struggle of our soldiers, we should respect the military leadership and its rule on secrecy, which are important in defending our country." No wonder the Senators who are currently looking into the wiretap scandal are livid. How can "Hello, Garci" a "state secret?" To my mind, such contention is shot through with absurdity!

The Senate has invited two former military generals to appear to give their testimonies, i.e., former AFP deputy chief of staff for intelligence and now the Western Command chief Rear Adm. Tirso Danga and former Chief of Staff Gen. Efren Abu. It is widely believed that Pres. Arroyo allegedly uses the military in subverting the will of the Filipino people in cheating her way to the presidency in 2004. This information was given by AFP Isafp agent T/Sgt. Vidal Doble, Jr.

Interestingly enough, one of the top generals being mentioned all this time is Gen. Hermogenes Esperon, Jr., the current AFP Chief of Staff who allegedly "participated" in the election irregularities. If there is more than a knee jerk or visceral frustration in the Senate, one could understand it.

Gen. Esperon defiantly declares: "Even if the Senate sanctions his men for their refusal to attend investigations of the "Hello, Garci" wiretapped tapes, they would remain unperturbed." "We would not attend Senate inquiries because the military leadership and its officers are not allowed even if there would be subpoenas issued," he emphatically warns.

Not all military officers participate in the reported election irregularities in 2004. Brig. Gen. Francisco Gudani and Lt. Col. Alexander Balutan defy Pres. Arroyo's order not to appear before the Senate. Both were then in the active military service. So it was understandable that the Armed Forces of the Philippines (AFP) appeals to the Supreme Court to sanction Gen. Gudani and Col. Balutan. The Supreme Court then decides that Pres. Arroyo, as the Commander-in-Chief, is justified in preventing both military officers from testifying.

In a recent Senate probe, the credulity of former Sgt Doble has been assailed by the administration senators. House Deputy Speaker for Mindanao Simeon Datumanong argues that Doble destroys his own credibility. He contends that "what we've seen grilled by senators was a man pushed by someone's political agenda and polished by money." Then he adds: "Sen. Miliam-Defensor Santiago for one alleged him to be a 'liar,' 'womanizer' and 'wife beater.' While Sen. Enrile cites a narration by Doble's wife Ariene in a kidnapping case she files against her husband that would prove that the former Isafp agent is lying when he claims before the House and later before a Court of Appeals justices that he is concerned about his wife and children's welfare."

But how about Gen. Gudani (ret) and Lt. Col. Balutan? How about the Marine Commandant Gen. Miranda (now detained) and the head of the Marine Special Forces Col. Quirubin (now detained). They had been all assigned in Lanao where the supposed "one-million-vote-margin" fraud and presidential election hanky-panky took place oiled by supposed multimillion grease money flown by a helicopter that landed in Iligan City airport? Do they have "credibility" problem, too?

View 51

Estrada: "Kangaroo Court Convicted Me."

Did the conviction of former Pres. Joseph "Erap" Estrada by the Sandiganbayan Special Division on plunder lucid enough for you? Or did it epitomize the wanton waste of justice?

His son, Senator Jinggoy Estrada and another co-accused in the "conspiracy to commit plunder" Eduardo Serapio, Pres. Estrada's lawyer were acquitted by the court. The sentence for Pres. Estrada: reclusion perpetua or life sentence.

What is interesting about this legal episode was the hype and the buzz, the inordinate amount of press-agentry and overblown publicity months, weeks and days before the actual handing of the decision. So much heightened fuss about the possibility of massive public demonstrations and possible military takeover since some disgruntled military officers, especially the junior officers would take advantage of the "volatile" situation! Or that the Communist Party would join in the fracas to topple down the Lady Chief Executive. The scenario being depicted before the verdict is "bloody" upheavals in the streets. It proves kaput. It is nearly a non-event. It is merely a clapped-out occurrence!

Salamat naman (thanks) no political or military upheavals took place. Not a bang but only a deafening whimper met the decision.

175

There are at least two possible reasons why no such "massive" demonstrations by the masses ever take place. One could be the fact that many Filipinos still believe that Pres. Estrada is really guilty of corruption and other political and moral transgressions. A family friend visiting from the Philippines observes when asked about the verdict. "Lahat naman silang (all of them are corrupt) politicians are corrupt, so what else is new in Philippine politics."

The second possible observation could be attributed to the fact that Filipinos are no longer committed to a worthy cause, whatever that means. The People Power spirit shown during the February 1986 EDSA peaceful revolution is no longer aborning in the hearts and minds of the Filipino people. Or could it be that the 1986 People Power was a fluke, a historical aberration, an accidental rendezvous with heroism (as described in my book: PEOPLE POWER; PROFILE OF FILIPINO HEORISM, which proves to be a runaway best seller in 1986-87). That people gather by the tens and thousands in EDSA because they knew that Pres. Marcos specifically ordered Gen. Fabian Ver "NOT" to shell or overrun with military force, especially the Marine and Special Forces Camp Aguinaldo where Gen. Fidel Ramos, National Defense Secretary Juan Ponce Enrile and Col. Gregorio Honasan are holed in. That when people hear this situation plus, of course, Jaime Cardinal Sin's supplication, imploring public support to topple down the Marcos regime, they all march to EDSA. This People Power peaceful demonstrations never took place in practically all major cities in the country. NOTE: except of course in Cebu where Mrs. Corazon Aquino and other politicians against Marcos have been having rally asking the people to boycott the Marcos government. But even then, the demonstration is not as big and dramatic as EDSA. I know because I am there. I join the rally with then Assembly woman Inday Nita

Daluz, the political campaign manager for Central Visayas of then candidate Corazon Aquino.

To expect EDSA People Power again would be asking too much, much too much for our people during this rationed time of economic distress and hardship. Especially when the prevailing notion among our people: "Pare pareho naman silang lahat!" (All politicians are the same).

Incidentally, did you know that two US warships, supposedly carrying guided-missiles, are anchored in Manila Bay? To "evacuate" Pres. Arroyo to the U.S. or another country should the political situation get out of control! This information has been reportedly tipped to Sen. Rodolfo Biazon, former AFP Chief of Staff and now chairman of the Senate national defense and security committee.

Now that Pres. Estrada has been convicted, just where do you think would the political orbit take our people and our country? Pray, kabayan. Pray!

View 52

"Blackmail Me, Blackmail You"

In analysis of any given situation, there is one reality one should always take into account. Concept is said to assume numerous forms. Conjunctive concepts, on other hand, are characterized by the simultaneous presence of two or more properties.

Viola. Philippine politics is no exemption. Take for example the case of Sen. Lacson who has been a pain in the neck of Pres. Arroyo. For one thing, the senator is fully supporting the move to re-open the "Hello, Garci" wiretapping controversy in the Senate. Obviously, Sen. Lacson's aggressive pursuit of truth is rankling the nerves of Pres. Arroyo. Imagine, Senate inquiry into a criminal act, i.e., cheating just to remain to be president of our republic, does not go away, which can consign the president into possible slammer. More than an emotional discharge, cheating to remain in power is a very serious act. It is not a mere political puny amidst the welter of endless accusations of irregularities in the Palace. Cheating in an election is a CRIME!

Naturally, it would not be a surprise if Pres. Arroyo and her disciples would launch counteroffensive moves. More than a plain-speaking threat, for example, Secretary of Justice Gonzalez along with Malacanang Legal Counsel Apostol has pointedly reminded Sen. Lacson that "even if he is a senator of the republic, he does not enjoy immunity from criminal suit." For bad or good, let us remind both these two ardent political mouthpieces of the lady Chief Executive that subverting the will of the Filipino people through phone instruction to one of the Elections Commissioners in May 2004 ordering him to "cheat" is a criminal act!

Sec. Gonzalez has warned Sen. Lacson and Sgt Doble that they could be charged with a criminal offense since "wiretapping is a criminal act." In addition, the Department of Justice argues that such revelation "will go nowhere as wiretapping is an illegal act and any testimony regarding it is not admission in court." Oh my, big deal. Such reasoning represents a fine-tune blackmail!

Another Malacanang move which has become a source of undiminished wicked pleasure was to remind Sen. Lacson that he could be investigated as a result of the Aragoncillo and Aquino convictions in the United States. In response to Sec. Gonzalez' blackmail through the filing of charges connected with the Aragoncillo espionage case, the Cavite senator dares Secretary of Justice to make good his threat if the Arroyo administration does have a case against him and other opposition leaders.

Refusing to remain sordidly silent on the Palace blackmail, Sen. Lacson snorts out loud: "Let him (Gonzalez) use whatever evidence he has. I have become too numbed over his constant threats. This is no longer nothing new,"

United Opposition president and Mayor Binay of Makati made a comparison between EO 464 (not allowing top government officials to testify in the Senate without the approval of the president) and the code of silence or "Omerta" of the Mafia criminal syndicate. "Executive Order 464 is nothing less than Omerta. And by again invoking EO, the Arroyo administration is acting like a criminal syndicate that is unwilling to cooperate with the pursuit of legitimate inquiries," Mayor Binay declares.

But there is no zig zagging about the Omerta code in the U.S. John Gotti who died in prison had been done in by one of his top crime lieutenants Gravano, who is also currently in jail. Whistleblowers are cheaper by the dozen when the pangs of guilt reign in. It could happen – and latest reports from the Philippines had it – that Filipino whistleblowers are coming out of the woodwork exposing government corruption.

View 53

International Poll Monitors Cry "Foul"

The Commission on Elections has started the canvassing for the senatorial and party-list elections. Certificates of canvass gathered by poll monitors from the countries Laos, South Korea, Cambodia, Australia, Slovenia, Poland, Hungary, Japan, Palau, Czech Republic, the Netherlands, Thailand, India, and Bahrain have been turned over to the National Board of Canvassers in Manila.

While the canvassing is underway, Mohamad Yunus Lebai Ali, a Malaysian lecturer and one of the monitors says "money to buy votes was handed out openly." He continues to say: "The transactions took place very blatantly. Our presence did not deter them at all."

The 210-member team from the Bangkok-based Asian Network for Free Elections (ANFEL) visit the six provinces of the Autonomous Region of Muslim Mindanao (ARMM) to witness the campaigning, voting and counting of votes. The international monitors say that unless changes take place in the manner of voting in the country, the credibility of Philippine democracy is "under threat in a region where powerful families still dominate politics."

The National Institute for Electoral Integrity (NIEI)) denounces electoral fraud and the use of violence and force in ARMM. Remember that in 2004, Pres. Arroyo won by a margin of one million votes in Lanao del Norte alone which become the controversial issue in the "Hello, Garci" wiretapped scandal. It could be possible that it is being repeated again this time around since the partial returns from the ARMM provinces showed Team Unity (TU of Pres. Arroyo is showing 12-0!)

NIEI Director Ali in a press conference on May 16, declares: "In terms of peacefulness, we all can agree that the atmosphere is not conducive for elections…I do not feel physically safe. What more about the voters?"

ANFREL Director Somri Hananontasuak of Thailand, underscores the presence of the military in polling centers "unusual and disturbing." She reveals: "There was deployment of military outside schools or voting centers. (In Thailand), we see them (only) in (instances of) national disasters and earthquakes."

There is one bright impression by a international monitor. One of them, Amin Shah bin Iskandor of Malaysia observes: "I am impressed" with the vigilance displayed by non-government election watchdogs National Movement for Free Elections (NAMFREL) and Parish Pastoral Counting for Responsible Voting (PPCRV).

In the meanwhile, GO spokesman Adel Tamano, accuses the Arroyo administration of orchestrating another cheating in the ARMM areas, which shows the two survey tail enders as the top vote getters in Mindanao: Luis Chavez Singson and Prospero Pichay. Tamano cries: "It's quite obvious the elections were rigged in ARMM. It is so statistically improbable for voters to vote 12 straight if you are going to vote."

Alarming trends are being noted in Manila. GO senatorial bets who are in the magic 12 earlier such as Francis Escudero, Manuel Villar, Panfilo Lacson and even independent Francis "Kiko" Panglinan land from numbers 13 to 16. In other areas such as Isabela and Eastern Samar the 12-0 vote for TU candidates was also assured. In

Southern Kudarat, out of 10,999 registered voters, 10,664 voted.

In another front, a ranking Comelec official who is earlier relieved by Comelec Chairman Abalos, Jr. is sacked when he questions the master list issued by the Comelec earlier. Comelec Director Fernando Rafanan, who is now on a "floating status" after serving as regional supervisor of the Comelec-National Capital Region (NCR), notes that the voters' list in the office of the elections officer does not tally with that of the listing held by the Information Technology department of the Comelec. "Our election officers and elections assistants are very frustrated about this." They thought that the de-listing by the Comelec is a success. But when the final list "is sent back to them, those that should have been removed are still included while those that should been included were missing."

With these developments, it is difficult not to evoke an irresistible, if disturbing vision that the 2004 electoral fraud engineered by Pres. Arroyo could be repeated. Are we Filipinos to continue to show a grand indifference to free and honest elections, the very hallmark of a true democracy?

View 54

Is The Glorietta Bombing A Diversionary?

Immediately after the Makati Glorietta 2 bombing in which 9 individuals are killed and more than 110 wounded, some members of the Catholic Bishops Conference of the Philippines (CBCP) have sounded the alarm calling for the resignation of Pres. Arroyo. Some key Catholic bishops express the suspicion that the bombing is a diversionary strategy of Malacanang Palace amid the mounting call for her stepping down due to series of corruptions stalking his government.

The Glorietta 2 tragic incident has only added fresh demand that Pres. Arroyo must make an exit. On October 21, CBCP public affairs chairman Caloocan City Bishop Deogracias Iniguez Jr. announces that the Catholic conference could either call a special meeting to take up the issue, or discuss it during its forthcoming general assembly.

Due to a litany of scandals in which Malacanang Palace has been implicated lately, i.e., ZTE National Broadband scandal, Cyber Education project questionable contract, among others, Bishop Iniguez Jr; Quezon City Bishop Antonio Tobias and Infanta town, Quezon province Bishop Emeritus Julio Labayen have demanded Pres. Arroyo's resignation. Their reason is that the Lady President has lost her moral authority. That such resignation at this time would prevent a "total collapse of the government." That for her to continue to stay in power would lead only to "national chaos."

The three bishops have issued a unanimous conclusion on October 20, in Quezon City ecumenical meeting: "If a regime is morally bankrupt, has propensity for falsehoods and repeatedly lies with impunity, there is no other alternative for the people but to demand that the leader, the Chief Executive, Commander-in-Chief, the President step down and resign." They elucidate further: "It is time for the sovereign Filipino people whom she has betrayed to now speak up as one voice and resoundingly ask her to step down."

In the meanwhile, Young Enlisted Soldiers Active and Retired Military Police for Solidarity (YES ARMS) spokesman Ismael Aparri appeals to the CBCP leadership to come out with a clear position on the resignation. This demand has assumed some degree of urgency particularly after former Catholic priest and now Pampanga Gov. Eduardo "Among Ed" Panlillo has revealed that he receives P500,000 cash after attending a meeting called by the President in Malacanang Palace in October 2007.

It would not be a surprise if any time soon, Pres. Arroyo would invite the CBCP leaders and members to Malacanang to be wooed, dined and to break one's fast, so to speak. Many suffering Filipinos perceive the Catholic bishops as a passive group willing to look the other way every time Pres. Arroyo commits government transgressions. This perception by the people has led to loss of many faithfuls, "not to mention the church leaders' loss of moral influence over their flock." Their view of the Church is laden with muted distrust. Is the Church listed in the cash register of the Palace? Many believe that every time Pres. Arroyo meets with the Bishops, she showers them with gifts, even cash, supposedly for the benefit of their respective parishioners.

Because of the past tendencies of the CBCP, some concerned Catholic faithfuls had shown cynicism, even suspicion, that the leadership of CBCP is in actuality in connivance with the Arroyo administration. That despite the blatant disregard of the rule of decency in public service by Pres. Arroyo, the Catholic bishops remain yielding and their "quietistic," and their que-sera-sera attitude is at best engrained – therefore, disturbing. Is this a somatological evidence of the co-existence between men of God and Lady of the morally vulgar and corrupt Palace?

Will the dining, wooing and wining days in Malacanang of the Catholic bishops over? Will the sweet smell of Malacanang "donation" to the bishops in the past come to pass this time?

Where is the CBCP when ten top cabinet members of Pres. Arroyo resign in disgust because of massive government irregularities and the "Hello, Garci" wiretapped scandal? The beleaguered Filipino people look to the Catholic bishops for moral strength and support in their demand for Pres. Arroyo to resign. But they are sorely disappointed. What is disturbing is the CBCP's call for the people "NOT" to go to streets to air their frustration and sense of government perfidy and treachery!

This time, however, there appears to be new ray of hope. After the Glorietta 2 bombing along with the recent government anomalies, some Catholic leaders are starting to voice concern which the Filipino people hopes would result in CBCP issuing a nationwide pastoral letter calling for the resignation of Pres. Arroyo. Or would it be another occasion when their hope would be dashed away again? Another shadowy piece of contemporary past of Church's betrayal passing through in a flash?

View 55

Distant Thunderbolt Of Civil War Being Heard?

The burden of choice of the military is becoming disturbingly clear: to serve or not to serve a Commander-in-Chief who is flaunting for all the Filipinos to see bribery taking place in Malacanang Palace. In the glare of TV and other media coverage, bagful of cash is brandished in the breeze of public eyes.

To this outrageous, if egregiously vulgar, display of Pres. Arroyo's lack of decency, there are now rumblings of possible civil war in the Philippines. No less than the Commandant of the Marines. Maj. Gen. Benjamin Dolorfino on October 10 sounds this dire warning: "a civil war is not far-fetched if the Armed Forces gets involved in an attempt to overthrow the government."

When the officers and men of the military learn of the "bribery" that took place in Malacanang during the President's meeting with no less than 190 congressmen and a number of provincial governors, sprucing up the image of the Lady Commander-in-Chief is a difficult task to accomplish.

What finally unravels Pres. Arroyo's proclivity to cheat, to engage in wholesale payoff of lawmakers and high government officials is the thousands of millions of pesos distributed among congressmen and provincial officials.

Gen. Dolorfino in a press conference held in Marines' Fort Bonifacio headquarters, issues an urgent appeal to all officers and men of the Armed Forces of the Philippines not to bet again on a military overthrow of the Arroyo government. He goes on to say: "Let's not gamble again. Next time, it will be a civil war. It is hard if people with guns are involved (in a military coup)."

Remember it has been widely reported in the Philippine media that the amount of the "bribe" ranges from P200,000 to P500,000. Gov. Eddie Panlilio, the priest who turned politician in Pampanga admits openly that he receives in cash P500,000 after attending the Palace conference. Bulacan Governor Joselito "Jonjon" Mendoza, brother of former Gov. Jose de la Cruz, also admits that he receives stash of crisp pesos totaling half a million. Congressman Antonio Cuenco of Cebu also acknowledges that he too receives a whole kit and caboodle of cash. He justifies it as Pres. Arroyo's "Christmas Gift." Hear this and hear it good, folks. The ever ebullient champion of the suffering kabalens Gov. Panlilio of Pampanga, the Catholic priest turned politician has now the temerity to give the "blessings" to such unrestrained propensity of Pres. Arroyo to buy politicians to stay in power. By exculpating the fellow kabalen, he is now – ex cathedra – giving "grace" to Pres. Arroyo's art of deception. In life as in politics, especially the Philippine kind, there is no such thing as free lunch. Pres. Arroyo has recently - and broadly - intimated that she would soon revisit the CHA CHA issue. With congressmen in her pocket, who would prevent her from convening a Constituent Assembly later? So she will stay in Malacanang beyond 2010. Who says only an ex-KGB Pres. Vladimir Putin of Russia likes to stay in power forever!. Also, the bogus "third impeachment" is like a dead duck now in Congress. Next attempt to impeach her (even with justifications) could not be filed until 2009! By then we may have a Parliamentary form of government.

If we talk of politicians amid the drumbeat of possible military coup, it could result – in the words of Gen. Dolorfino – in less disastrous political upheavals. But if we talk of "disgruntled" military officers (especially the junior officers) and men, well it would be different. It certainly could provide a richly detailed synopsis of possible "civil war" as envisioned by no less than the current Marine Commandant. The former Marine Commandant Maj. R. Miranda is now in jail since he is suspected of masterminding the failed military coup of February 24, 2006.

Just how "disgruntled" are some segments of the military? In a frantic attempt to woo the military, Pres. Arroyo announces recently that she would be increasing by P150 day the troopers' combat duty pay. But the disturbing fact is that the soldiers have not received their expected increase; that even their combat pay has as yet to be received.

And the politicians receive recently thousands of millions of pesos for just attending a Palace meeting while the soldiers are dying in many a battlefield! Weaving the staying power of Pres. Arroyo in Malacanang is becoming increasingly difficult to contemplate at this point in time.

View 56

Keep Them In Public Payroll

This "Hello, Garci" ghost continues to bedevil Pres. Arroyo. And it will continue to be so since the Senate is doggedly determined to find the truth.

And Malacanang is frantic, scarred like hell. Why? Because there is a possibility that the Lady President could finally be exposed which could eventually consign her to prison.

No wonder, Pres. Arroyo is doing everything to stymie, stonewall, and if possible, prevent outright the Senate to summon government officials who know something, or allegedly involved in the "Hello, Garci" wiretap trickery.

The Palace would do practically everything under the sun to thwart, baffle and frustrate any attempt to expose Pres. Arroyo's poll chicanery.

Just exactly how the Palace go about it? Consider, if you must, the latest antics and ploys of the alleged "cheating" lady president. Because the current AFP Chief of Staff, General Esperon Jr is reported to be one of the "Hello, Garci" generals mentioned in the wiretap, he plucks from retirement Adm. Tirso Danga, the ISAFP (Intelligence Service of the Armed Forces of the Philippines) head when the controversial tape phone calls between Election Commissioner Garcillano and Pres. Arroyo supposedly took place. Despite Adm. Danga's precarious health, he has been appointed as "special assistant to the National Security

Adviser to the President." Presto, he is now in the government service again. Had he not been appointed to the position, Adm. Danga could be summoned to testify before the Senate. Now he is shielded from the investigatory reach of the Philippine Senate! And even if he is forced by the SC to testify, Adm. Danga (and Gen. Esperon) could invoke: "We will not testify since "national security" is involved!" Why, even a knucklehead and a moron know that "Hello, Garci" is a criminal act.

Another stonewalling attempt by Malacanang. Two retired CA Associate Justices appeared before the Supreme Court recently to argue that the Senate must not be allowed to proceed from its "Hello, Garci" probe.

Senior Supreme Court Associate Justice Angelina Sandoval-Gutierrez pointedly asks petitioner former CA Justice Oswaldo Agcaoili if he would be financially affected by such on-going Senate hearing. And if he is, how much would be the amount of financial damage. Justice Agcaoili tersely replies: "none."

This was followed by another comment bordering sarcasm: "What was your injury or interest in this bitter scandal when your name was not even mentioned in the controversial tapes?" SC Justice Sandoval-Gutierrez observes bitingly: "It should be President Arroyo and (Comelec Commissioner Virgilio) Garcillano who should file the suit."

Just exactly what the two retired CA justices are against the Senate? Listen, and listen to this please: "They were petitioning the Supreme Court not to allow the Senate to play the entire "Hello, Garci" tapes!" Whoa. Another argument by these former CA justices: Playing of the tape constitutes an "illegal disbursement of (public) fund." But SC Associate Justice Gutierrez reminds that "the Senate is mandated to conduct an investigation in aid of legislation." End of the story of impertinence!

View 57

Demand For Impeachment Until One Is Blue In The Face!

In our country, one can attempt to impeach Pres. Arroyo for her alleged political sins until he or she is blue in the face and nothing could come out of it.

Pres. Arroyo is now immunized against any attempt to kick her out of the Palace through impeachment at least for another year. On November 12, 2007, the minority members of the House of Representatives walk out of the impeachment House hearing being conducted by the Committee on Justice. They charged that the hearing is a sham. A political charade. In storming out of the hearing, Rep. Roilo Golez, one time National Security Adviser by no less than Pres. Arroyo, declares: "We do not want to be part of it." In a burst of disgust, United Opposition (UNO) leader Adel Tamano takes more than a swig of anger when he says that "with all due respect, it's really a trap. I have been a professor for long, and I can sense when there is a trap."

Lawyer Roel Pulido first files an impeachment complaint which is according to opposition camp is an attempt to insulate Pres. Arroyo from a real, valid, and genuine impeachment complaint. On November 12, by a 29-7 votes, the Committee on Justice headed by Quezon City Rep. Matias Defensor, says that the amendments to the impeachment must be first received by the House Secretary General and transmitted to the Speaker who should then refer the case to the Rule Committee, which in turn would refer it to the Justice Committee. By going through this channel, the impeachment would be considered a "new" complaint. As such, it would have to wait till next year for its filing in the House of Representatives.

But Tamano argues that since the new impeachment complaint is not a new one but a supplement to the Pulido complaint, it should be submitted direct to the Justice Committee.

What does the "new" and "genuine" impeachment supplement consist? Bayan Muna Rep. Teddy Casino declares that the supplement is a "genuine impeachment complaint." which alleges that Pres. Arroyo has committed culpable violations of the Constitution, betrayal of public trust, bribery, graft and corruption and other high crimes due to her alleged involvement in extra-judicial killings, among others.

There are no less than 110 pages in the supplement complaint It is deemed to be the "strongest and most substantial yet against Pres. Arroyo." However, it has been junked like shards of irrelevance. On November 14, the Justice Committee panel has voted 43-1 declaring that the supplement impeachment complaint of the opposition is "insufficient in substance." And yet, the supplementary complaint, which is strong because it contains a litany of evidence that would support the impeachment of Pres. Arroyo has been jettisoned and junked by Pres. Arroyo's alleged recipients of bagful of cash for "lack of substance." Money talks.

Albay Rep. Edcel Lagman, a die-hard Arroyo partisan and vice chairman of the panel, declares that the "accusation against Mrs. Arroyo is hearsay and could not meet the requirements of Section 4 Rule III of the Impeachment Rules." Hearsay? Are we Filipinos numbskull and meatheads and all to believe Rep. Lagman!

Despite the walking out of the opposition lawmakers, Rep. Defensor provides a window of opportunity for the eventual impeachment of the lady president, when he observes that the opposition must need to secure the support of 80 congressmen if it wishes to reverse the committee's decision and refer the complaint to the Senate for trial. In the meanwhile, UNO spokesman Tamano plans to take the case to the Supreme Court. In the same vein as Caesar's analogy, we Filipinos, both abroad and in our country can collectively declare: "render the impeachment unto GMA what is GMA's render unto Filipino nation."

View 58

Junta Governance: Not Quite A Creative Alternative

Are they punch-drunk power hungry groups who are demanding that Pres. Arroyo, Vice-President Noli De Castro. Senate President Manuel Villar, House Speaker Jose De Venecia resign? That all should have the elementary decency to leave their positions and give way to the "junta" leadership. A transition which would usher in a new government free from the political trammels and turmoils of the present corruption-laden Arroyo government. This proposed transition junta would be headed by Supreme Court Chief Justice Reynato Puno. A novel political idea?

This is the brainchild of the Kilusang Makabangsang Ekonomiya (KME), which is headed by Jaime Regalario, with support from former Vice-President Guingona, three Catholic Bishops Julio Xavier Labayen, Antonio Tobias, and Deogracias Iniguez, along with some civic and business leaders. Had it been tested before. Yes, if you recall what happened to Bolivia, when the Chief of the Supreme Court assumed national leadership in transition due to fractious political wrangling among the top Bolivian leaders.

If in fact this "transition junta" takes effect, it is necessary that the transition leaders being groomed by KME must be willing to accept the national leadership. But it is now clear that Chief Justice Puno pooh-poohs the idea. In turning down the offer, Justice Puno, through his official spokesman, thanks the group. He says that he is not interested in politics. His love is foremost of all is to remain head of the Supreme Court. His goal: to safeguard the independence and integrity of the judiciary. Well taken.

In the current crossroads of Philippine politics, the image of the Supreme Court is also tarnished. For the Chief of Justice to head the government is a hard sell even if Chief Justice Puno did not say: "Thanks, but no thanks!" As a matter of fact, Justice Puno's rating has nose dived like that of Pres. Arroyo in recent national polls. His rating reflects a picture of a double-dealing genre of quasi-judiciary.

In fact, many view the current Philippine Supreme Court as a political tool of Pres. Arroyo. In a kaleidoscopic flashback, one recalls that the Supreme Court, under the leadership of Chief Justice Hilario Davide, Jr. with Supreme Court en banc, which incidentally included Reynato Puno, swears in rather hurriedly then Vice President Arroyo as president when in fact there "is no vacancy in the Office of the President." Many consider such hurried swearing in as a constitutional anomaly itself. It has been surmised that it was carried out "while a coup d'etat was being mounted by the elite civil society and the military chief of staff along with service commanders (in) January, 2001."

Let's remember that reworking our current Constitution that comes into being in 1987 would be a hard sell even by an aggressive high-pressure salesman. Under the 1987 Constitution, the line of succession is clear cut and sharply outlined. If Pres. Arroyo resigns, Vice-Pres. Noli de Castro assumes the presidency. If due to some fortuitous events both Pres. Arroyo and Vice-Pres. De Castro resign, Senate Pres. Villar will, by operation of law, become the president. Within 45 to 60 days, special elections for the presidency and vice-presidency would be held.

If one considers the constitutional rules, then the Chief Justice of the Supreme Court is not a constitutional successor. It is therefore a wise move on the part of Chief Justice Puno to turn down the offer of the KME.

In the meanwhile, there would be in the coming days, weeks or even months wearying, if exhausting, string of heated debates on the issue of "transition junta." Why? Under the Arroyo government there are scandalously layered of unresolved corruptions, i.e., the Joc-Joc Bolante Fertilizer bad, suffocating odor, North Rail Project never-ending allegations of payment of grease money, Diosdado Macapagal Highway robbery, Jose Pidal scandal, ZTE National Broadband caper, along with the latest Malacanang Palace cash giving, aka bribery. Of course, the "Hello, Garci" wiretap scandal, which remains an eyeball-gougingly offensive since Pres. Arroyo allegedly steals the presidency from the late presidential candidate Fernando Poe, Jr.

View 59

Supreme Court No Longer Daydreaming

It now appears that highest court of our land is no long engaged in some kind of legal daydreaming or mystical fantasy as regards a host of extra-judicial slayings of the critics of the Arroyo government.

It also seems to suggest that the Supreme Court is hell-bent on curbing the killings of the leaders and followers of human rights groups and other opposition organizations in the country allegedly perpetrated by the military. In a two-day summit on extra-judicial killings, Associate Justice of the Supreme Court Antonio Carpio comes up with a worthy of praise suggestion. He submits a proposal which has been unanimously passed that the Supreme Court adopt a rule, which would allow individuals threatened with extra-judicial slayings, whether by state security agents, national police operatives, insurgents or any other groups, to "apply for protection order from the courts, which would direct the National Bureau of Investigation (NBI) or police to provide them security."

Aware that such extra-judicial murders happen, regardless of the place or group, the SC makes it clear that such protective action is extended to tribal councils whose customary laws are recognized, and to churches along with non-governmental organizations with their consent.

Out of the 12 groups that attend the summit, 3 groups agree to support the recommendation that there be a three-year ceasefire agreement between the government forces and the communist group to allow both the warring parties to talk peace with the aim of ending the insurgency problem. On July 16, 2007, AFP Chief of Staff Gen. Esperon, Jr. also suggests a three-year ceasefire to find a viable solution to the festering problem of extra-judicial killings.

That is a nice prescription. Anything to end these unsolved slayings is to be praised. But what is perplexing is that the same Gen. Esperon who ponderously blurts not too long ago that the extra-judicial killings are perpetrated by the leftist or communist group to "purge their ranks."

So if in fact that these leftist groups are responsible for the murders of their own "scawalag members," what assurance then that the killings will stop during the 3-year ceasefire when the government forces are not responsible for the slayings? Charm-struck or not by Gen. Esperon's initiative, let's hope that we will not find our expectation hanging of the sleeve of false hope!

View 60

Economy, Economy, Economy

Faced with a bright, seemingly endless and enticing armamentarium of forecasts, charts and diagrams before the May 14 election on the redolent and imagistic picture of our "robust" economy, Pres. Arroyo has instructed all his Team Unity (TU) senatorial candidates not to engage Genuine Opposition (GO) senatorial aspirants in a debate or debates if the topic is not "economy, economy, economy."

With rather insularity of boastfulness bordering on arrogance, the Lady President announces that "our economy" deserves attention and appreciation. No politicking, please. And so be it. If in the debate the GOs would confront the TUs on the issue of extra-judicial killings of civil rights leaders and advocates, journalists critical of the administration and more especially on the "Hello, Garci" wiretap controversy, there would be no debates.

Always at the edge of political gobbledygook, Pres. Arroyo insists on discussing our present state of economy. Like a proud peacock displaying her plume worthy of admiration, the Lady Commandeer-in-Chief has her final say. And so there has been no debate.

Humbled and defeated in the recent mid-term senatorial election, but still walking jauntily, after all she has a Ph.D. degree in economics, she is in recent days faced with a constellation of bad economic news. Upon realizing that she is again caught in the act of hoodwinking the Filipino people, she fires last week the Commissioner of the Bureau of Internal Revenue (BIR) Jose Mario Bunag. The reason, tax collection has plummeted during the first semester of this year. Fall guy walking! How did we know it? Who announces the depressing economic news? Not Pres. Arroyo. Malacanang is quiet like a quiet one feels before a tornado. (I should know because our home in Indianapolis, Indiana, years ago was hit by a tornado).

SOLUTION NUMERO UNO: The government would have to sell state assets in order to avoid "bloating the budget deficit, which has already approached P53 billion "or 84 percent of its target budget gap this year" (in the first six months). Secretary of Finance Margarito Teves admits that "privatization of the state-owned assets might be the only way to stop the deficit from ballooning, and simply because relying on pure tax collections, to reduce the revenue shortfall would not do it." Teves says that the target collection in 2007 for the Bureau of Internal Revenue is P730 billion; for the Bureau of Customs: P228 billion.

SOLUION NUMERO DOS: Borrow, borrow, borrow. No wonder, the benchmark interest rates have taken a dramatic increase. The rate for the 91-day T-bill took a dramatic upswing last week to 3,477 percent from 2,996 percent during the last auction on May 23, or a 48.1 basis point increase. The reason for the current economic downturn in our county: The investors are worried about our economic posture.

Another dark economic cloud hanging in the Arroyo government horizon: Last Friday, due to the Estrada decision jitters, the Philippine Stock Exchange index slipped 43.48 points or 1.114 percent to 3,758.84. The all-share index also lost 24.10 points or 0.99 percent at 2,411.33. If Pres. Arroyo is so bad in diagnosing the economic health of our country, would she be able to convince a Peeping Tom to buy her Windex merchandize?

View 61

Gloria: The Wizard Of Ooophs

If the results of the May 2007 mid-term election are not enough to unearth the deep-rooted and nearly uncontainable rage and rejection by our kababayans of Pres. Arroyo, wait for a new round of political developments soon to unfold. Just consider, if you must, her own cabalens rejected her two hand-picked gubernatorial candidates. Why two? She wanted to be sure that the cabalens would not elect an opposition candidate, who happens to be a priest. It is lamentable that Pres. Arroyo suffers a political black eye in her own political bailiwick; in the land of her beloved father, former Pres. Diosdado Macapagal. Not too long ago, her half sister implores her to step down for her sake, her family and the country. She ignores her.

Then there is Senator-Elect Antonio "Sonny" Trillanes, whose fellow Magadalo mutineers have demanded in 2003 that she should step down because of blatant corruption. Sen. Trillanes demanded also Gen. Angelo Reyes and Gen. Victor Corpus to resign. Interestingly enough, Gen. Reyes has supposedly been "booted out" as Secretary of National Defense (but immediately offered him a powerful cabinet position) and Gen. Corpuz "retired" from the service. Two weeks after the Oakwood Magdalo military "revolt," Asia Pulse reveals the results of the survey on the people reactions to mutiny. "More than 55% of the Filipinos supported Trillanes' Magdalo mutiny! More than four years in a Marine brig, Trillanes ran as a senator. It was the political miracle in contemporary Philippine history. Trillanes' election is particularly foreboding for Pres. Arroyo. As a senator, he will team up with the "band of brothers" (all PMA graduates), i.e., Sens. Biazon, Lacson, and Honasan in dredging up previously ignored corruption charges against her. Remember the Jose Pidal money laundering probe, along with the Philippine Charity Sweepstakes Office (PSCO) and the Philippine Amusement and Gaming Corp. (Pagcor) investigations on allegations of these agencies having used their funds to help underwrite the candidacy of Pres. Arroyo in 2004 along with the senatorial candidates in her camp. It is now obvious that despite the massive government funds used to drum up support of the Team Unity senatorial candidates in 2007, it went crashing down the tube of utter rejection.

And now the impending verdict on the plunder case against then President Estrada. Waiting for the decision would not have generated some political furor this week. But last Wednesday,July 3. full-page ads appeared in all major national newspapers in our country. It was entitled: "ERAP; GUILTY OR NOT GUILTY. KAILANGAN BANG MAY GULO?" (DO WE NEED TO HAVE DISORDER).

One must recall that a few weeks ago, the plunder case is submitted for decision after oral arguments are made. The Sandiganbayan is mandated by law to make a decision within 90 days. Three-months period would allow the Sandiganbayan to come up with a verdict. But why the sudden publication of newspaper ads?

One church leader, according to reports from Manila, has beem informed by Pres. Arroyo that Erap would be "convicted." Does this mean that Pres. Arroyo has ordered Sandiganbayan to "find Pres. Estrada guilty?"

In calling up images of Philippine contemporary political history, Pres. Arroyo would find herself in a discomfiting or uneasy chair if the detained Estrada is found "NOT GUILTY!"

Then her presidency would serve as a bastardization of our Constitution insofar as the transition of presidential power is concerned. Certainly our Philippine Permanent Representative to the UN Ambassador Davide would be closely watching the developments as they evolve. Why? As Chief Supreme Court Justice, he allows himself to give legitimacy to the illegal assumption of the presidency by then vice-pres. Arroyo. As a reward, he is enjoying his position as our UN Ambassador. Opposition leaders are trumpeting in Manila that Ambassador Davide's position is a "reward." They ask: Why the rush to judgment? No wonder, detained Erap is still contending that he is still "the president" of the Philippines.

At times, her own top political lieutenants are to blame for the negative perception of the president. Imagine in the light of the ads published in all national newspapers. Executive Secretary Ermita has the following statement as quoted by the media: "The court has spoken. Due process has been observed. Justice has been served." One does not have to be living under the cave of Mt. Makiling to deduce or conclude that a decision of "guilty" has been made by the Sandiganbayan. No wonder the persona of Pres. Arroyo as a "cheater," "corrupt," and "vindictive" and these adjectives need no further explanation why her popularity is sliding precipitously.

Pres. Arroyo claims to high heavens that her government is transparent. Well, in the name of true transparency, the newspaper publishers and editors must now reveal the identity of those who place the full-page ads. I may not be a lawyer, but I consider Sec. Ermita in contempt, since he violated the sub judice legal rule. Why would the ads declare: "Let the rule of law prevail." But a decision as to the guilt (or its absence) is yet to be released by the Sandiganbayan. Follow me as I present my take in a somewhat politically ravishing manner. If a decision has already been made, then reminding the people that the "court has spoken" would have rationale. Is this Arroyo administration revealing or riding on the dreamlike dance of brazenness? "Erap: Guilty or not guilty. Kailangan bang may gulo?" That question leaps beyond politics. It certainly leaps into fear that the decision could trigger mass demonstrations. Remember, Gen. Esperon orders joint military-national police deployment in many "poor" neighborhoods in Manila and Makati! Why? Manila is under an opposition Mayor Alfredo Lim and Makati has Mayor Binay. Both cities could be the flashpoints of massive demonstrations once Erap Estrada is found guilty.

View 62

Adrenaline-Juiced Paranoia?

Is our President Gloria Macapagal-Arroyo suffering from some kind of political psychosis which is characterized by undue fear that her alleged cheating and lying would be exposed should there be a formal investigation in the Senate? That if an independent Senate enquiry is held, the naked corruption perpetrated during her leadership could be found being handed on the fingernails of major scandal. She does not, of course, want to go through the labyrinth of exposure. And people's condemnation.

On August 7, 2007, Senate President Manuel Villar, Jr. announces that the new chairman of the Blue Ribbon Committee would be the neophyte Senator Alan Cayetano. Why is this important appointment be worthy of notice. Well of all the senate committees, the Blue Ribbon has an extraordinary power to initiate investigations of the executive officials, Cabinet members and it includes the top lieutenants of Pres. Arroyo.

It was not a secret that for weeks Sen. Lacson is interested in becoming the chairman of the Blue Ribbon committee since he knows that through such vantage position, he could launch needed investigations on the alleged anomalies which involve Pres. Arroyo and her key Palace and Cabinet members. Pres. Arroyo is virtually mortified at that prospect. She starts to throw her weight around to prevent Sen. Lacson from ever becoming the Blue Ribbon chairman. Obviously, Pres. Arroyo has prevailed. The question is why would the appointment of Sen. Alan Cayetano be considered less ominous by the president? For one thing the neophyte senator from Pateros, Rizal, is viewed by Malacanang as less gung-ho in finding a treasure trove of scandals and corruption in her government. However, it is too early to find out whether Sen. Cayetano would prove a toothless kitty cat or a ferocious tiger who would doggedly pursue investigations of the government anomalies. But remember that it was the Rep. Alan Cayetano who "exposed" the supposedly "secret" bank account of the First Gentleman in a Swiss bank. Later, it was found out that then Rep. Cayetano had no basis for such allegation. I believe Sen. Cayetano and play it up in one of my columns. My apologies, Mr. Arroyo.

Let's go back to the Senate Blue Ribbon Committee. While other committees in the upper chamber could call for an investigation under the blanket cover of "in aid of legistation," even when in the end no legislation has been approved, in any of the Blue Ribbon investigation the "approval" of Pres. Arroyo is needed under the "gag order." The justification given by Malacanang is that such requirement would give a long lead time.

The gag order is first embodied in the infamous Executive Order 461, which is struck down by the Supreme Court earlier. But it has been replaced by another order she issue at a later date, i.e., Memorandum Circular 108, which is further strengthened by another Executive Order by way of insuring that no documents from the Palace and other executive agencies are released without first securing the approval of Pres. Arroyo.

Imagine if the object of the investigation involves corruption in the Palace, or cheating in the elections, and other anomalies in the executive branch which could eventually involved the President, would such Malacanang permission be given to the summoned executive officials to testify under oath in the Blue Ribbon Committee?

With Sen. Lacson out, and Sen. Cayetano in, could Pres. Arroyo enjoy now a more politically balmy weather in her remaining three years in Malacanang Palace?

View 63

So What Else Is New?

The latest poll survey which has been released on August 1, 2007 by IBON Foundation indicates that 72% of the Filipinos are "dissatisfied" with the performance of Pres. Gloria Macapagal-Arroyo. But whatever happens to her "vision" of a better life for our people since she stubbornly claims that under leadership "social payback" is a reality. What a wanton waste of reason and rationality. Bribe payback, yes. Social payback, no.

The IBON Executive Editor Rosario Bella Guzman reads the results of the survey as follows:

a. Three-fourths of Filipinos rate themselves as poor, with 76.8 percent of the respondents indicating they have difficulty paying bills, up from the figure of 67.6 percent in January and 69.3 percent in the same period last year.

b. Forty four point 35 percent of the respondents state there are not enough available jobs and livelihood opportunities in their area. Thirty two point 66 percent say there is none at all while 16.95 percent state there are enough job and livelihood opportunities.

c. The respondents also states that it is becoming increasingly more difficult for them to pay for the basic expenses, especially for the purchase of medicines, medical treatment, water bills and electric bills. The breakdown as regards their inability to pay the basic necessities of life: electricity and/or water (72.45 percent); medicines and/or medical treatment (71.24 percent) children's schooling (67.74 percent); food (67 percent); and transportation(65.32 percent).

Malacanang must be imbued with a distorted sense of reality. When reminded that not only the IBON but the Social Weather Stations and the Pulse Asia surveys indicate that the Filipino people have a high disapproval rating of Pres. Arroyo, the Malacanang sycophants, those nearly blind, servile self-seeking flatterers shamelessly intone: "the presidency is not a popularity contest." One does not need to feel a primal sense of economic deprivation to come to conclusion that it's pure bull kind of argument!

Hey, guys people are feeling the pangs of poverty. It is no popularity contest.

As regards Pres. Arroyo's SONA speech in which she claims that our economy has improved, the overwhelming majority of the Filipinos think that she is engaged in some shadow boxing. To put it bluntly, she is lying again.

Just exactly why more than 11 million of us OFWs are working in many countries in the world, if jobs are aplenty and quality of life is as rosy as what Pres. Arroyo is claiming in our country. Pres. Arroyo is so used in lying that to be honest about it, she could tell a lie quite graciously even in shackles and blindfolded.

View 64

What's The Meaning Of 11,138,067 Votes?

None, zilch! That is if you subscribe to the stand of the Department of Justice as regards the case of Sen Antonio Trillanes IV who is now languishing in the Marine detention cell despite winning the senatorial election last May 2007.

Oh, where is democracy in our country if being duly elected by more than 11 million Filipinos do not mean anything. Are we to eradicate the fundamental suavities along with high purpose of democracy based on the people's mandate?

So what is the legal impediment why Sen. Trillanes could not discharge his responsibilities as an elected senator of our country. The Arroyo government argues that Senator Trillanes is "guilty" of rebellion for having led 30 junior officers and 300 soldiers in staging a "mutiny" at the Oakwood Condominium in Makati in July 2003.

The case in now with Makati Regional Trial Court (RTC) presided by Judge Oscar Pimentel. On July 25, Trillanes petitions the court to allow him to discharge his duties as a duly elected senator. Judge Pimentel junks the petition on the ground of "lack of merit."

In the wake of this new decision by the Makati Trial Court Judge, many supporters of Sen. Trillanes have organized a letter-writing campaign. Many student leaders, religious groups, as well as members of the academe along with Filipinos from all walks of life have signified their intention to join the "letter-writing campaign." The target is to get more than 11 million votes symbolizing the votes cast in his favor to pressure the court to allow Sen. Trillanes to attend the senate sessions. The Department of Justice strenuously opposes Sen. Trillanes petition by citing the case of Zamboanga del Norte Rep. Romeo Jalosjos who was convicted in early 1970s of raping an 11-year old girl. While in jail, Jalosjos petitions the court to allow him to attend the House of Representatives. It was not granted.

But the case of Sen. Trillanes is different. He has yet to be convicted. Are we not supposed to be considered innocent until proven guilty in the court of law? When the people's mandate is denied, simply because of some twisted political considerations cloud the minds of some government officials, which could very well include Pres. Arroyo, then such government reckless proclivities serve as a stain in our democracy. Then our government is moving our democratic beliefs to warp speed of irresponsibility.

View 65

Peso's Rally "Worrisome"

On Monday, June 4, 2007 the peso hit all-time high in terms of peso-US dollar exchange: 45.83 to a dollar. Good or bad for our economy?

It appears that there is one aspect that bothers Bangko Sentral ng Pilipinas (BSP) Gov. Armando Tetangco Jr. After the dramatic upswing of peso in the last few days, Tetangco finally admits that this development is a source of worry for the government. He says: "There's a bit of concern with the rate of appreciation, which may cause volatility and lead to some disruptive effects." He adds that "we prefer to see an orderly adjustment."

The peso-dollar exchange keeps on changing faster, it seems, than one who rotates tires for a living. And this growth of peso is hurting the OFWs who are now according to latest economic report remitted more than US$14 billion in 2006. And it will continue to increase since many Filipinos will join the exodus for abroad in search of the pot of gold at the end of the rainbow of employment.

If this seemingly breakneck speed in the rise of the peso will not be checked, the OFWs will continue to get hurt, according to Sergio Ortiz-Luis, treasurer of the Philippine Chamber of Commerce and Industry.

In addition, the Central Bank is ready to fire a warning shot. The rise must be monitored. If not, it will hurt our Philippine economy over a long haul.

The reason: In the last few months, several exporters of local products and commodities are experiencing some economic pinch. For example, no less than 720 companies under the Philippine Exporters Confederation of Cebu (Philexport-Cebu), an association of local exporters, made a strong appeal to Pres. Arroyo seeking assistance.

Jay Yuvallos, president of Philexport-Cebu, claims that 35 furniture companies have closed down their operations as result of the strong peso. This means more than 50,000 persons had been laid off. Yuvallos warns of more mass lay-offs and company closing down if the pesos continues to strengthen against the dollar.

Filipino traders and exporters announce that they are losing billions of pesos each month due to the strong currency as locally-made goods become more expensive to foreign buyers. Sergio Ortiz-Luis Jr. estimates that the export industry lost a total of P4.5 billion since the pesos started to spiral upward to 45 per dollar level. These losses, according to him, were the result of "foregone orders and missed opportunities." Local exporters, mostly small and medium sized firms have even stopped taking new orders at the current exchange rate.

Is the rise of the peso value a sign of the Arroyo administration's handling of the economy? Before the May 14, Malacanang Palace had been touting the economic progress under her sound economic policy.

The reason for this rather "abnormal" rise in value of the peso is due to "speculation" rather than improved economic conditions, Ortiz-Luis observes that "It will end when the speculators have stopped selling their dollar reserved."

To solve this "abnormal" rise of peso, let us interrupt this endless stream of speculations.

View 66

"Deteriorating," Madame President!

On May 2, 2007, the United State Department got unsettling news for Pres. Gloria Macapagal-Arroyo. She is presented with a new banquet of accusatory and disturbing messages. Under her watch the press freedom in our country is fast "deteriorating." Now the Philippines has gained a new notoriety when it comes to Filipino journalists exercising their profession not only being muzzled but actually being murdered. The Philippines has joined the "club notorious" when it comes to press freedom. The other members which are known to suppress freedom of the press are Afghanistan, Venezuela, Pakistan, Russia, Egypt and Lebanon, to mention a few.

The U.S. State Department observes: "We are... concerned about increasing limitations on press freedoms around the world. In many countries, governments are tightening libel laws, media ownership is increasingly controlled by governments and pro-government forces, the number of independent press outlets is declining, restrictions on Internet search engines and the rights of citizens to express themselves freely over the Internet are multiplying, and those who try to independently seek, receive or disseminate information and ideas are being persecuted."

The blunt message to Pres. Arroyo: "let the endless stream of murders of Filipino journalists stop. The extrajudicial slaying of Filipino journalists seems to be taking an upswing trend.

Other countries being identified by the U.S. State Department monitoring unit. These are Burma, Eritrea, North Korea, Equatorial Guinea, Cuba, Iran, Turkmenistan, Tunisia, Uzbekistan, Syria, Belarus, China and Zimbabwe.

The Reporters without Border continues to accuse the government of Pres, Gloria as trying to stop the press from doing its job of "safeguarding democracy" It also says that the Philippines as the most dangerous country for journalists to practice their profession after Iraq. With such a damning critique, let the Arroyo's thread of repression continue to tremble in the air!

The U.S. State Department reaffirms its commitment to uphold the right of journalists to ferret out the truth. Freedom of the press is a key component of democracy. Both U.S. Department and Reporters without Frontiers latest analyses make a bumptious revelation of the sorry state of journalism in the Philippines under the watch of Pres. Arroyo.

View 67

Idiot Is As Idiot Does

Poor Gloria! Like a soggy turon wrapper being swept away by the Binay swirling political floodwaters in the last few days, Pres. Gloria Macapagal-Arroyo makes a last-ditch attempt to save her administration's political face. Malacanang blinked and blinked like a blind dog looking for some tainted pet food.

One does not have to be a Ph.D. holder in economics to know that what happened to Makati Mayor Binay is a political idiocy carried to the nth level. First she orders the 1) suspension of Makati Mayor Binay, 2) garnishment of all Makati City assets and property, and 3) freezing the personal bank accounts of Mayor Binay and his vice-mayor days before the May 14 elections. If this is not pure political harassment, what is?

As one would know, Makati under the watch of Mayor Binay, the president of United Opposition against Pres. Arroyo, has been a pain in the behind of the Arroyo administration ever since 2001.

Then the mind-blind stupid Malacanang operatives surrounding Pres. Arroyo must have realized the gargantuan political misstep they have committed. As a result, Pres. Arroyo on May 5, 2007 ordered the 1) deferment of Mayor Binay's suspension, 2) lifting of the BIR order to garnish all the Makati City bank assets, and 3) unfreezing Mayor Binay's personal bank accounts and other property.

217

Will this make the indefatigable Makati mayor happy? Nope. You bet. Mayor Binay is now fighting back like there is no tomorrow. He reveals that the Palace Rasputin behind all this political fiasco is PAGCOR Chairman Ephraim Genuino, reported to be a money "bagman" of the First Couple. As you know, two of his sons, i.e., Anthony and Erwin are running as councilor in the First District and Congressman of the 2nd District of Makati, respectively. Genuino is the Numero Uno political enemy of Mayor Binay.

Mayor Binay has called mass rallies to denounce Pres. Arroyo's Nazi-style leadership. Imagine, even his private home in San Antonio has been surrounded by some National Police and military contingent. Even some members of the Presidential Security Command of Malacanang are reportedly serving as "bodyguards" of the Genuino sons in their political barnstorming.

Mayor Binay comments on the government order: "Our situation is similar to the garnishment of our bank accounts. Without access to funds, we cannot provide basic services. Now, without a local chief executive, basic services and city government operations are affected." And also, he adds: "Makati is not facing any threat of terrorism and we do not have any history of election-related violence. So what is the reason for the presence of these armed policemen and Malacanang PSG?"

Pres. Arroyo must be squirming in Malacanang right now as this Binay flop is whirling around her. This "Makati Revolt" could spread around the Metro Manila, then surrounding provinces and, lo and behold, could spawn throughout the country. If it does, Pres. Arroyo's bets' chance of victory especially her senatorial candidates is placed in grave jeopardy. Pay close attention on the senatorial elections. It is a political referendum on Pres.

Arroyo, who according to latest polls, is DISTRUSTED by a great majority of the Filipino people.

Of course, there is the negative international ripple effect. Foreign governments are justifiably alarmed about this latest display of arrogance of power of the Arroyo administration. They are already concerned with the seemingly unabated slayings of journalists, leaders of the civil rights movements and her political opponents. This Binay's bizarre political zarzuela of the absurd makes them doubly concerned. As regards these killings, Comelec Chairman Abalos, Jr. is asking the people to "pray for the repose" of the victims of violence." Says he: "I have just called for additional troops, and still the political killings continue, what do you want us to do?" Resign, perhaps!

It has been learned recently that more than 200 foreign observers would be in the Philippines to monitor the elections. The foreign poll monitors will be coming from Australia, New Zealand, Singapore, Japan, Great Britain, Canada, Sweden, Finland, Germany, France and the United States, to mention a few.

If there should be a massive cheating like in May 2004, then there is only one solution left for our people: REGIME CHANGE!

View 68

RP Is A Corrupt Nation For Nothing

Imagine if you must, that you were nominated for a cabinet position that requires confirmation by the Commission on Appointments. If you were ready to put a finishing touch to the presidential appointment, or if you think that it is a slam dunk sure that you will be a cabinet member, think again. Vanish that notion.

It has been revealed by no less than our Speaker of the House, Jose de Venecia, who is alleging that extortion money is being asked by some members of the Commission on Appointments (CA) for the needed confirmation. If you think that it is a farcical production of a malicious mind, think again.

You will recall that Domingo Panganiban, chairman of the National Anti-Poverty Commission, alleged that some members of the CA had approached him and tried to exact money from him in exchange for his confirmation as then secretary of the Department of Agriculture. Now, Sen. Lacson is demanding that Panganiban come out with names who are involved in the CA "scandal." The Cavite senator announces: "I think in due time they will have to name names because they started accusing some members of the CA, particularly members of the House of the Representatives." He is not only referring to Panganiban but also Finance Secretary Margarito Teves and his father, Negros

Occidental Rep. Herminio Teves, who exposes the alleged CA extortion scheme. It is hoped that such allegations would bring into orbit of possible investigation. If it is true, then it would provide a portrait of congressional decay or freezer burn.

Who could be the legislators-of-the-moment involved in this disturbing corruption? If you ask Senator Miriam Defensor Santiago, there is nothing that could come out of any investigation. She doubts if something revelatory would ensue from such inquiry into the "racket." Sen. Santiago claims: "Extortion, like bribery, takes place only between two people, and one of them has to testify for the charge to stick. Generally, no nominee will incriminate himself by testifying that he obtained confirmation by giving a bribe, an appointment or a contract to a CA member." That statement serves as more than a classic coy morsel of Philippine politics. So with that frame of mind, let bribery in the CA go its own merry way. Lamentable.

What is a Commission on Appointments (CA)? It is an independent government body. It is composed of 24 members, i.e., 12 from the House of Representatives and 12 from the Senate. It can promulgate new rules and guidelines insofar as its administration and operation.

Sen. Lacson in the light of these allegations, proposes that CA members would be barred from speaking to any Cabinet nominee. As it stands now, Sen. Lacson adds that "unethical as it is, there are no existing rules barring that. The act of seven (members of the CA) talking to a nominee should be made punishable." He mentions particularly the amendment that now prohibits CA members from invoking Section 20 of the body's rules on the last day of the Congress' session or before it goes on sine die adjournment.

This time. Sen. Santiago is backing up the idea of Sen. Lacson. To avoid further erosion of the trust of the people in CA, Sen. Santiago demanded that there should be a needed change. She cites: "Under the notorious Section 20, it takes only one CA member to veto all the rest of the 23 other members. This one-person veto is what empowers a CA member to extort bribes, government appointments or public works contract in exchange for confirmation."

Viewed in this light, one could then assume that our current Philippine Permanent Representative to the United States Ambassador Hilario Davide did not bribe any CA member since he did not receive the official confirmation from assuming his current position in New York City's UN Headquarters.

What is Pres. Arroyo's reaction to the CA scandal? Press Secretary and presidential spokesman Bunye states that Pres. Arroyo should not be "dragged into the issue." But she is our president and this is happening under her watch!

View 69

Is Military Coup Brewing?

According to latest post-election political bites from our country, it appears that a possible military coup is looming. Whether our pipeline in the Philippines is correct or not, it is worth our while to wait and see. And if there is going to be one, we hope it is only a rumor howling to the moon since our country, our people can ill afford such a political cataclysmic flare up. It is like our kababayans are asking for a hole in the head. Foreign investments would dry up should there be one.

But, and it is a big BUT, some segments of the military hierarchy are conducting an in-house survey on the sentiments of the rank-and-file of the military. There are questions being asked framed in seemingly harmless manner. The one question being asked of the soldiers and officers: "Do you agree, or disagree, that the electorate gave former Navy Lt. SG Antonio Trillanes IV the vote to openly express their disappointment with the current national leadership, which is Gloria Arroyo." Bad piece of news for our Lady Commander-in-Chief.

Why would such a question be asked of the officers and men of our Armed Forces of the Philippines at this juncture? If we were keen enough in our observation, we will come up with a conclusion that because of the results of the May 14 mid-term elections, i.e., the opposition GO candidates practically slam in the face of our president the reality that the Filipino people mistrust her and she has lost the confidence of the Filipino people.

In the latest military survey, there are several "trick" questions, which appear harmless and innocuous but pregnant with possibility of some convulsive events in the offing. Hear this. If a politician wants to feel the pulse of the people, it is OK. But if a military starts going around asking soldiers questions such as: "Whether the votes cast in favor of Trillanes reflect the people's trust in his competence for good governance." This is followed: "Whether soldiers perceive Trillanes who is a military man, to have limited knowledge of governance."

Whether we end up on the side of the political prophet or not, the material thing that we the civilian, both in New York, New Jersey and elsewhere in the world, can ask: "Why are some military brass asking the ordinary foot soldiers such questions? Hear this and hear this good. The question is framed so carefully to include the word "military" and "competence for governance" of Trillanes as a senator-elect.

The young senator-elect, who is currently detained in a military jail, is not going to be responsible for "governance." So what is the rationale for asking his "competence to govern our country?" He is a senator who is essentially a legislator. Senators come and go but they never played a role in "governance." Passing laws, yes. But never governing our country! Why then ask the soldiers this question? Could this be a precursor to eventual military takeover by some military top honchos once the survey results indicate that a military man, like Trillanes (for that matter Honasan) has the ability and competence for national governance In the political parlance, it is known as "testing the waters."

Obviously, Senator-elect Trillanes is now serving as a lightning rod, so to speak. Is his election a mirroring of the possibility that a military top brass wearing a white hat riding on a white horse will come galloping to Malacanang Palace soon? Another question that could raise some eyebrows: Has the election of Trillanes indicate "a compelling desire for change in the military and Defense establishment," which is followed by another baffling question, i.e., does the Trillanes victory "imply" defiance of the AFP top brass?

To measure military pulse by reading the military opinion poll is entirely different from measuring the public pulse through public poll. The former is ominous in the wake of the post-election developments.

Do you still recall the "Hello, Garci" wiretap? Several military generals (some of them are retired now) were mentioned as receiving instructions on how to rig the results of the election in favor of Pres. Arroyo. At least two generals who supposedly took part in the "cheating" are still very much in the service of Pres. Arroyo, i.e., Lt. Gen. Hermogenes Esperon, now the AFP Chief of Staff, and Lt. Gen. Hermogenes Ebdane, now the Secretary of Natonal Defense. If I were in their shoes, I would be worried sick!

Reason: The "Band of Brothers" in the new Senate will be initiating investigations of some accusations against Pres. Arroyo. The Band of Brothers is composed of Senators Lacson, Honasan, Biazon and Trillanes, all PMA alumni. They already announce that they would revisit some charges of corruptions against the Arroyo administration, i.e., Fertilizer scandal, the jueting-gate and of course the "Hello, Garci" controversy, to mention a few. The train of the Senate would-be investigations would gather momentum and will go on chugging happily along if Sen. Lacson becomes the Chairman of the Senate Blue Ribbon Committee.

Last week Comelec Commissioner Rene Sarmiento announces that the 2004 massive fraud supposedly engineered by then Comelec Commissioner Virgilio Garcillano should be "revisited."

Pres. Arroyo, we would like to say at this point, is not a cheater, or even a touch of a cheater, or not much of a cheater, but her refusal to cooperate to open the seven boxes of evidence now in the House of Representatives, which are already gathering cobwebs, I am afraid we might be forced to conclude that she is indeed a "cheater."

View 70

A Promising Future Has Been Shattered

In my recently released book, I relay to Pres. Arroyo my dismay the fate of Leandro Aragoncillo, an ex-marine, who worked for both Vice President Dick Cheney, former Vice President Al Gore, and former President Bill Clinton.

Primarily because of his past impressive associations as well as his unblemished military credentials, the United States Federal Bureau of Investigation (FBI) has employed him as an analyst. For a Filipino-American, this certainly is a remarkable and pride-enhancing achievement. The future is ready for his taking. He literally could ride to the moon! And now, suddenly, the bloom is off the rose. Sad. Unfortunate.

He has recently been found guilty of espionage by the court. His sentence" 10 years in jail" in a plea bargain. In defense of his passing secret U.S. documents in his attempt to topple down the Arroyo government, he informs the court that "I am just trying to help bring Filipinos out of poverty." He adds: "I never intended to cause harm or injury to the United States."

After he stole the information, and after downloading it, this supposedly intelligent ex-marine, obviously performing his military service with testosterone-fueled devotion to the United States, actually e-mails the said dossiers to opposition leaders in the Philippines. Both ex-President

227

Estrada and Sen. Lacson admit that they did receive such e-mails.

I further inform Pres. Arroyo that American media coverage has never mentioned "top military secrets" involving the United State policy over the security of the Philippines. The United States-Philippine military relations have never been compromised. It appears only that the onus of controversy is not on the nature of the dossiers, but more on the reflection of Pres. Arroyo's sagging popularity. So why the conviction? The U.S. intelligence community is not overly concerned with the dossiers, but more with the embarrassment Aragoncillo has caused the White House and the FBI.

Aragoncillo must have detested the layer upon layer of wholesale cheatings and ballot riggings (remember "Hello, Garci"), which Pres. Arroyo appears to have flawlessly orchestrated.

View 71

Smell Of Censorship?

Something disturbing is looming in our country! And it is hoped that it is not true. But with our country under the watch of Pres. Arroyo cum some worshipful fanatics around her, I would not be surprised if my forthcoming book is not welcome in our country. That there is a strong possibility based on the following latest incidents that my soon-to-be-released book: THE RISE AND DECLINE OF PRESIDENT GLORIA MACAPAGAL-ARROYO is going to be banned in our country.

I make no apologies in saying that it is an adrenaline-juiced book severely criticizing the Arroyo administration. But if what Pres. Arroyo has said during the recent media forum attended by Filipino and foreign journalists that the Philippines "is one of the most democratic countries in the world" is in fact true, why then some sweaty die-hard Arroyo political operatives in the Mailing Department of our Philippine Senate would resort to committing some despicable behavior that smacks of a repressive regime?

Consider the following latest incident: Yesterday, April 24, 2007 I received through the US Postal Service (not UPS or FEDEX) a package with a big note: "RETURN TO SENDER, ADDRESS UNKNOWN." What say that again? I sent the package almost a month ago which contained the galley proof of my book through Johnny Air office adjacent to Krystal Restaurant in Roosevelt Avenue, Queens. My instruction was to hand deliver the package to Senator Alfredo Lim to his Office in the Philippine Senate in the GSIS Building in Pasay City. Aside from the usual fee, I paid an extra $5.00 so that a Johnny Air special courier will personally deliver the package to the Senate.

How come when I opened the unexpected package I found my letter to Sen. Lim in the original envelope I used, along with the original package containing the galley proof of the book I found a handwritten note: "PLEASE DELIVER FOUND IN STREET."

This was the second time it happened to my package that I sent months ago to Senator Lacson. Johnny Air has informed me then that "Senator Lacson Office "refused to receive the package...that Sen. Lacson's driver returned the package to their Makati Johnny Air branch office.

Let us assume that an addressee found the package as a "nuisance mail." Like all "nuisance" mails or package we receive in our mail, we just throw it to the waste basket. But the latest incident must be sending me a message that any "criticism of Pres. Arroyo is not allowed" particularly if it is a book.

Look what happened to Ninez Cacho Olivarez, the Editor and Publisher of Daily Tribune. She is now charged with "sedition." Her only crime: being critical of Pres. Arroyo's government. As a matter of fact, her newspaper's office has been raided and thoroughly ransacked by the National Police along with some military contingent last year. Why?

And our Lady Chief Executive boasts that our country is "one of the most democratic countries in the world!" It is a rank hypocrisy. It is a stone-faced lie!

It appears now that in our country, once you give money to the poor, you are an angel. They might even vote for you. But once you ask them why they are poor you are committing a seditious act! Worst, they can put a label on you: You are a communist, a leftist, a Party-list politician. I wonder what the Arroyo political and military die-hard subalterns living in the marble temple of power in Malacanang Palace, would accuse me when my book is finally released and distributed through WWW AMAZON.COM and WWW BARNESNOBLE.COM. Will they charge me of sedition? Will they accuse me of being a Communist? Oh, what a slithering political snake this Arroyo government which seemingly enjoys bathing in the waters of abusive and repressive regime.

View 72

What A Grotesque Statement!

"The Philippines Is The Most Democratic Country
In The World."

Guess who said it last week before the international media forum attended by foreign journalists? Pres. Gloria Macapagal-Arroyo, that's who! It is one of the heavies of her bald lies. Such a statement is an affront to reason and probity.

The United Nations (UN) Human Rights Commission rapporteur Philip Alston who has conducted an investigation of the extra-judicial killings of journalists, judges, lawyers, bishops, human rights advocates, even labor leaders last year, reveals that he has a copy of ll0-page document of the Republic of the Philippines Order of Battle (OB), which is the hand maiden of the military. The military is obviously using it to eliminate through extra-judicial slayings the "enemies" of the state!

Of course Pres. Arroyo could deny knowing the military OB, but at the rate she has been singing praises of the military, one would not believe such denial.

But supposed, for the sake of argument, that she really does not know the OB, then one can come out with an argument that she is really not in full control of the military. Then what kind of Commander-in-Chief is she?

One would remember that in the May 2004 presidential elections, Pres. Arroyo lost substantially in Metro Manila where slum and squatter dwellers live. Since the party-list candidates have their constituency in these areas, she orders deployment of military troops ostensibly to maintain "peace and order." What peace? What order? The reason is simple which does not defy any rationality. She wants to show military force to intimidate the voters in the forthcoming mid-May 2007 elections not to cast their votes to party-list congressional candidates, which the military tags as a "communists" and "leftists."

When the dwellers of these slum areas complain to the media, Pres. Arroyo through his chief aide, Executive Secretary Ermita, a retired military general himself, urges the Armed Forces of Philippines (AFP) leadership to set a date for the withdrawal of the army troops in these deprived areas. To which Gen Esperon, Jr., the AFP chief, answers that the soldiers would be withdrawn only for one day, i.e., on the day of the Election, May 14. and only if their "projects" would have been finished by then. What "projects?" Full implementation of a pile-driving intensity of intimidation and harassment of the voters so they would not be able to votes for the party-list candidates?

The Catholic church is asking her to withdraw the military ominous presence; the Commission on Elections is also urging the military to leave the place; many human rights groups are urging the military to leave; even Malacanang Executive Secretary expresses concerns over their presence in these slum areas, but the military likes to stay and it will stay. No buts or ifs about it. But can the top military generals disobey Pres. Arroyo, the Commander-in-Chief? Good question. Obviously yes. The President, poor lady Commander-in-chief, appears to be unable to rein in the army. The military generals control the military, period. Democracy you say? We know that her own very survival as

President depends on the protection of the generals that she appoints. No more glancing gaze on the role of the military in our government which is progressively sinking into authoritarian, militaristic rule.

View 73

Another Impeachment Attempt

"Impeach President Gloria Macapagal-Arroyo!" Again? Is this to be another piteous wail of desperation by opposition legislators in the House of Representatives? Will this once more turn into a spectacle of political horse-trading and a last-minute betrayal? It's my hope that this roar for impeachment will not end in another whimper.

Representative Francis Escudero, House minority leader, declares that this second time around, the impeachment initiative will be "fully activated." If GMA impeachment were a detergent, the opposition would announce it as a "new and improved, reconstituted" product. The boyish-looking House leader roundly criticizes the many opposition representatives who become the early eager beavers supposedly determined to impeach the president, but who, when the time comes to vote, simply evaporate into thin air.

What else is new in politics—the Philippine kind? I come to the conclusion that Pres. Arroyo has blown the administration House members the kiss of money. Pardon my words; I like to be blunt. Bribe money freely fly over the cuckoo's nest of Philippine politics. Even the dullest political observers will be tempted to think so. Even the political eggheads will find no difficulty in thinking so.

In a raw, crudely sketched, political morality play, no fewer than four opposition lawmakers who promise that they are committed to seeing the impeachment of our lady president through to the end did not appear on voting day. There appears to be a failure of true commitment. Obviously, President Arroyo is delighted with these modern-day Filipino political Houdinis—these busy political elves who disappear into the never-never land of Philippine politics.

Rep. Escudero mentions this disturbing scenario in the House of Representatives during the canvassing of votes. He alleges that there is vote switching and ballot box snatching in the Batasan, which favor Pres. Arroyo. Never mind "Hello, Garci." Pay no heed to Gen. Gudani's accusation that vote riggings had taken place in Lanao in 2007. This supposed cheating has taken place in the hallowed halls of Congress. But the barrier between accusing and proving is a big hurdle.

If the opposition leaders, however, turn out to be unable to prove such an accusation, the 'reactivated, reloaded and enriched" impeachment initiative could very well be smashed to smithereens.

If however, those members of the House who witnessed the alleged ballot swapping and other anomalies in the Batasan in the 2004 presidential election, find in their hearts even a scintilla of conscience, a tiny spark of conviction, then and only then will this second attempt to impeach the president have a fighting chance of being successful.

Or if one morning, some political supporters of Pres. Arroyo in the House wake up to the snap-crackle-and-pop of guilt, then our president is in trouble.

If the latest Supreme Court decision finding some crucial and controversial portion of the 1017 emergency declaration unconstitutional, maybe the opposition lawmakers will have some political traction. Or if the political allies of Pres. Arroyo in the House know of the alleged anomalous ballot box switching and vote shaving, and know that it is being masterminded by moneyed and highly-placed political lieutenants of the president, perhaps there is justification for the renewed optimism among the authors of impeachment. If not, the dreadfully overwrought attempt to impeach Pres. Arroyo might remain in the realm of the preposterous. If the Escudero opposition camp is able to present convincing and compelling reasons for impeachment, then the scaffolding of indifference might collapse.

Okay, let's assume, for the sake of argument, that Pres. Arroyo is found guilty as charged and that the verdict is impeachment meted out by the Senate, who will then be our president? If we stick to the Constitution's clause on succession, Vice-President Noli de Castro will be our next president. Many political pundits, leaders of business, industry, and banking sectors, academicians, effete elites, and ordinary Filipinos think, rightly or wrongly, that he hasn't the intellectual wherewithal to be an effective president of our republic. Unfair to assume, but political reality sometimes bites deeply.

It is possible that Filipinos might reason as follows. "Between President Arroyo and Vice-President De Castro, the former is much better than the latter whose claim to prominence, many Castro-phoebes think, is due merely to his ability to read teleprompters."

Is it possible that for this reason, the impeachment of Pres. Arroyo will not come to fruition? Does one need to be a Cassandra to foresee what will happen after Pres. Arroyo's exit? In the meanwhile, citizens of the Philippines are helpless to do anything. They are just—pardon my words—merely salivating and waiting.

Author's Other Books

Call for True Democracy: Letters of an America-Educated Filipino To President Gloria Macapagal-Arroyo

The Rise and Decline of President Gloria Macapagal-Arroyo (most recent)

People Power: Profile of Filipino Heroism

The Aquino Administration: Baptism of Fire

Education in the Life of a Foreign Exchange Student

Asian Immigration to America

Foreign Medical Graduates in America

Filipino Physicians in America (two volumes)

Political Participation of International Physicians in America (with Antonio Donesa, M.D.)

His forthcoming book, entitled: *Philippine-American War, 1899-1902: A War America Refuses to Remember*